PUFFIN BOOKS

YOU ARE SIMPLY PERFECT!

Sadia Saeed is a psychologist with over two decades of experience of working with schools, corporates, child guidance centres and hospitals. A TEDx speaker, Sadia is the founder of Inner Space, a mental health platform that focuses on psychotherapy, teaching self-awareness and wisdom programmes, and training organizations in mental health and wellness practices. Her core approach to mental health and emotional resilience rests on cultivating a deep understanding of one's own nature, creating space for personal growth and change, and developing compassion for oneself and others.

ADVANCE PRAISE FOR THE BOOK

'We all need to learn to identify with our goodness, our wisdom, our confidence: this is the key to success. Sadia's advice helps all of us—not just young people—do exactly that! I rejoice'—**Venerable Robina Courtin,** an ordained Tibetan Buddhist nun and a student of Lama Yesha and Lama Zopa Rinpoche

'Universal compassion, driven by wisdom, is the leading panacea for the world—this is the quintessence of Sadia's book. I deeply appreciate the author for bringing this legacy before the world'—**Venerable Geshe Dorji Damdul,** Director at Tibet House, New Delhi, Cultural Centre of His Holiness the Dalai Lama

'A remarkable exercise in the development of self-awareness for the youngsters through stories and Buddhist psychological techniques of mindfulness, involving listening, reflecting and meditating that will help dissolve the negativities of their limiting thoughts, emotions and actions'—**Renuka Singh,** professor of sociology, JNU; and director of Tushita Mahayana Meditation Centre, New Delhi

'Sadia brings a rare combination of empathy and experience to her writing, drawing from decades of her work as a therapist. What becomes clear from the first page onwards is that she really cares about people. This is a book I would pick for my loved ones—and for myself—as a guide to mindful living'—**Taran Khan,** award-winning author of *Shadow City: A Woman Walks Kabul*

'Recasting the idea of "friendship" in a radical way, this book unfolds a profound truth—that we can be friends with the world, if we first truly learn to befriend ourselves. Artfully, compassionately and in deceptively simple ways, Sadia shows us how to do that. In doing so, she speaks to the hidden pandemic of our times—anxiety and depression, especially amongst our younger generations'—**Shabnam Virmani**, film-maker and founder, Kabir Project

'Even though this book is a must-read for teens, it speaks to all of us who want to befriend and love ourselves. Through everyday stories and simple exercises, it demystifies self-love as a practice that we can get better at by taking small little steps every day. The gentle words and insights make you want to hug yourself after every few pages!'— **Namrata Rao**, award-winning editor and director

'The book is well-written in easy steps for the reader to follow. *You Are Simply Perfect!* is a much-needed guide for teenagers and adults alike—so much of who we are is conditioned, leaving our minds restless. Mindfulness, if practised sincerely, can have enormous benefits in bringing clarity and peace to the inner being—and I would strongly recommend that the contents of this book be integrated in our daily life practices. Sadia, your clarity of thoughts flows through beautifully and makes me glad that you decided to pen down your insights and share it for the benefit of others'—**Upasana Saraf**, head HRD and psychologist, Bombay Cambridge Gurukul

'A practical book that integrates Buddhist wisdom with contemporary life in a simple and accessible format. Sadia's experience as a psychologist reflects in the pragmatic and reader-centric approach used in the book. Her writing style is warm, non-formal and is aimed for a young reader. However, the book has a universal appeal and adults will have much to gain from it as well. The reader will especially benefit from the practices of meditation and mindfulness described in relation to dealing with difficult emotions'—**Nivedita Chalil**, PhD, founder: ARTH (counselling and arts-based therapy)

'Sadia Saeed's book *You Are Simply Perfect!* is the calming balm every teenager needs. It engages them to think deeper, accept themselves and grow through this process of thought and reflection, rather than talk down to them. It introduces practices of meditation and mindfulness that I hope will guide readers through their lives'—**Saumya Roy**, author of *Mountain Tales: Love and Loss in the Municipality of Castaway Belongings*

YOU ARE
SIMPLY
PERFECT!

A MINDFULNESS AND SELF-AWARENESS
GUIDE FOR TWEENS AND TEENS

SADiA SAEED

Illustrations by **SHRiNEH NAMDEO**

PUFFIN BOOKS
An imprint of Penguin Random House

PUFFIN BOOKS

USA | Canada | UK | Ireland | Australia
New Zealand | India | South Africa | China

Puffin Books is part of the Penguin Random House group of companies
whose addresses can be found at global.penguinrandomhouse.com

Published by Penguin Random House India Pvt. Ltd
4th Floor, Capital Tower 1, MG Road,
Gurugram 122 002, Haryana, India

First published in Puffin Books by Penguin Random House India 2021

ISBN 9780143446156

Book design and layout by Samar Bansal
Typeset in Futura BT by Manipal Technologies Limited, Manipal

www.penguin.co.in

To the Buddha, and to all sages,
sufis and gurus, known and unknown.

To Dad, for sowing the seeds of love,
compassion, introspection and poetry.

CONTENTS

Introduction   xi

Note to Parents/Guardians   xv

How to Use This Book   xvi

PART I: MAKING FRIENDS WITH YOURSELF

1. Are You a Friend to Yourself?   3

2. Mindfulness: How It All Started   7

3. Pleasure vs Happiness: Choosing Wisely   16

4. To Understand Is to Love   26

5. Gentle Effort Is Key   34

Practice Summary   53

PART II: MAKING FRIENDS WITH YOUR MIND

1. Beginning to Explore with Your Mind   61

2. The Mind—a Storyteller   70

3. Negativity Bias: Looking for Negatives   79

CONTENTS

4. Your Thoughts Are Not Powerful; You Are!   81

5. How to Handle Difficult Thoughts   84

6. Metta: A Powerful Antidote for the Judgemental Mind   88

Practice Summary   96

PART III: MAKING FRIENDS WITH YOUR BODY

1. Connecting with the Body   103

2. Supporting the Body   110

3. Body Scan Practice: Relaxing and Noticing the Body   114

Practice Summary   118

PART IV: MAKING FRIENDS WITH YOUR FEELINGS

1. Understanding Feelings   125

2. Our Usual Way of Dealing with Feelings   129

3. A Wise Way of Working with Difficult Feelings   136

4. The Importance of Noticing Pleasant Feelings   145

Practice Summary   146

PART V: DEALING WITH SPECIFIC EMOTIONS AND DIFFICULT SITUATIONS

1. Dealing with Anger   153

2. Dealing with Boredom   163

3. Dealing with Anxiety   170

4. Dealing with Jealousy   181

5. Dealing with Body Image Difficulties: Learning to Love Your Body   188

CONTENTS

6. Understanding and Working through Addiction   202

7. Understanding Bullying and Dealing with It   218

Practice Summary   245

The Path Ahead   247

References   249

Acknowledgements   250

INTRODUCTION

When I was in my early teens, just like you, or any other adolescent, I faced my share of struggles. These included crushes and rejections, the pressure to study harder, boundaries set by parents that seemed unreasonable and unfair, insecurities about how I looked, and fear of judgements from my peers and teachers.

When I look back now, I realize that talking to someone older, wiser and relatable would have been very helpful. Someone who would have offered a different way of looking at life, a better understanding of the situations I was facing, and some constructive methods to deal with them.

I hope through this book, I can be that person for you. I understand your struggles. I have been your age. I have also worked as a psychologist with people your age. I know you don't have it all easy.

But I can tell you this: a lot of your struggles will definitely ease off. They will pass. Some of these difficulties will even make you stronger and more courageous. Most importantly, I want you to know that there are ways to understand and manage the challenges that you are going through. There are tools and techniques that you can use and ways through which you can train your mind to deal with them.

Around 500 years ago, Sant Kabir, a mystic poet from Varanasi, said, '*Pothi padh padh jag mua, pandit bhaya na koye / Dhai aakhar prem ke, padhe so pandit hoye* (O people, you read so many books, but none gets wise; the wisest is the one who learns the language of love).' Bulleh Shah, a Sufi poet and philosopher, said something very similar: '*Padh padh ilm hazaar kitabaan, kadi apne aap nu padhya nahin / Jaa jaa wardey mandir maseeti, kadi mann apne wich wareya nahin* (You have studied a thousand books, but not tried to really study yourself. You have entered so many mosques and temples, but have never tried to enter your own mind).'

What are these wise sages trying to convey? That we human beings have become experts at gaining knowledge of the outside world. We have, however, not even made an attempt to really look within. We are not seeing our inner world; the world of our thoughts, feelings and memories. This is a world of our fear, anger, jealousy and sorrow. It is also the world of our joy and happiness.

I had my first real glimpse of this inner world when I started meditating. By then, I was already a psychologist working for several years. As a psychologist, I knew all about helpful and unhelpful behaviour patterns, thoughts that I should focus on, and those that I should not believe in. Even then, I did not understand how to simply and practically approach my thoughts and feelings. I did not know that I could watch them, accept them, and that there was a way to look at them kindly and work with them in a wise and peaceful way. I have learnt that through my mindfulness and meditation practice over the years.

This is the method and the understanding that I am sharing with you through this book. You are about to take on this most precious journey into yourself. Some learned people have gone so far as to say that this is the only real journey in life that is worth undertaking.

So, dive in and explore this mindfulness guide to your inner world. It will help you truly understand yourself and connect with the joy that is already inside you. This book will help you relax, slow down, turn inwards, and remain ever aware and kind to yourself. It will also help you deal with the day-to-day challenges that you face in life.

Lastly, if you feel ready to do so, invite your family or friends to go through this book with you. It is a beautiful journey to take together with loved ones.

NOTE TO PARENTS/GUARDIANS

If you are a parent/guardian and are considering buying this book for your child, be prepared for a transformative journey yourself. While the book is written for your child's age group, the universality of the concepts and practices apply to every human being. Going through this book with your child will help you form a stronger bond, which comes from sharing wisdom practices together.

As adults, we have learnt certain fixed ways of being, thinking and behaving that are actually quite unhealthy. We now need to work on unlearning some of the unhelpful tendencies that are deeply ingrained. Children, on the other hand, are still learning the ways of the world. My hope is that this book will help your child learn fruitful ways of working with their mind early in their lives, so they don't have to go through the cycle of learning and unlearning.

Try to understand this book along with your child, concept by concept and practice by practice. However, please try not to advise your child to follow this book. Instead, share your own learnings and experiences—what you resonate with, what you find confusing, what is becoming clearer, what anecdotes you relate to and so on.

The idea is not to push your child to follow these practices but to inspire your child by following them yourself. Children who have parents/guardians who practise mindfulness and make it a part of their lives, turn to it in times of stress, even if they cannot immediately relate to the ideas.

I wish you all the very best and a lot of wisdom and joy on this journey together with your child.

HOW TO USE THIS BOOK

You Are Simply Perfect! is written with the sole intention of helping you make friends with yourself. In order to do that, you have to observe, understand and accept different aspects of yourself.

The book is divided into five parts. The first four parts contain concepts and practices to help you learn mindfulness so you become familiar and friendly with your mind, body and feelings. In the fifth part, I have explained how to work with specific challenges that you might face in life like anxiety, addiction, bullying and so on.

These concepts and practices may be very new for you. So to help you make the most of this book, here are some suggestions on how to use it.

- Read it slowly, a little bit at a time. Try to think about what you have read and how it applies to your life. Only then move to the next bit.
- Each part contains practices to do alongside your reading. In addition, there are several reflection exercises with space provided to put down your thoughts. It is best to do these practices and exercises as and when they occur in the book.
- Before immersing yourself in the practices, let your family know that you will be meditating for a few minutes and you'd need to be by yourself.
- At the end of each part, there is a practice summary, in which the practices you need to be following regularly are set forth. Just stay with those practices. When you finish the

next part, start following the practices mentioned in the practice summary of that particular part. For instance, when you finish Part I, follow the practices mentioned in the practice summary section of Part I. Those are your daily practices until you finish Part II. Then graduate to the practices that are in the practice summary of Part II and let go of the practices mentioned in the Part I practice summary.

- There are reflection spaces provided at the end of each part. You can use them to put down any interesting insights you may have had, notes that you want to remember, page numbers you might want to refer to again. You could also use it for doodling or in any creative way that is relevant to your learning.
- Highlight or underline the passages you find helpful. Come back to them several times, especially because sometimes reading the same piece again can make it clearer and give a better perspective.

Above all, enjoy the practices and the time spent in silence. May this book be beneficial to you.

PART I

MAKING FRIENDS
WITH YOURSELF

1

ARE YOU A FRIEND TO YOURSELF?

Since this entire book is about being a friend to yourself, let's try and understand what being a friend means. So I checked for the definitions of the word 'friend', and here are some:

'A person who has a strong liking for and trust in another person'—*Merriam-Webster Dictionary*

'A person who you know well and who you like a lot'—*Cambridge Dictionary*

And here is a definition by Winnie the Pooh that I liked the most:

'A friend is someone who helps you up when you're down, and if they can't, they lay down beside you and listen.'

Going by these definitions, a friend is a well-wisher—someone who knows you, trusts you, cares for you and most importantly, listens to you and tries to understand you.

Ask yourself the following questions:

- How often do you relate to yourself in this way?
- How often do you listen to yourself?
- Do you try to understand yourself?
- Are you kind to yourself when you are down or upset?
- Do you try to know your thoughts and feelings?

This kind of friendship with oneself is rare.

Making friends with yourself is similar to making friends with someone else. When you want to be a good friend to another person, what do you do?

You hang out with that person. You spend time with them and listen carefully to what they have to say. As you pay attention to what they are saying, you learn more about them. You begin to understand them and feel for them. Slowly, your friendship grows stronger.

Such a wonderful thing! A feeling of deep friendship, a special bond.

You need to do the same for yourself. Do you relate to yourself in this way? Do you spend time with yourself trying to understand and know yourself?

When you are by yourself, especially when you don't have to study or do an assignment, chances are you listen to music, watch TV, play a game or spend time on social media.

You are distracted by things other than *yourself*. You are not really spending time with *you*. Whenever there is nothing to distract you, you feel bored. You don't really like to be with yourself. Your friendship with yourself is not very strong.

However, there is nothing to worry about. Most of us are the same. Very few of us know how to stay peaceful and joyful by ourselves, without distractions.

But this book is here to change that! With the help of the ideas and practices that you will find in the following pages, you will be able to build a loving and healthy friendship with yourself.

And the most important practice that will help you do so, is the practice of mindfulness.

What is mindfulness, you may ask? Let's first do a practice to experience what it means to be mindful.

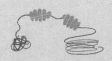

MINDFULNESS PRACTICE: KNOW THE SOUNDS

Read the guidelines below and then begin your practice.

Take a minute to experience all the sounds that you can hear right now. To do this well, close your eyes for a bit and focus on these sounds.

It does not matter whether you like or dislike the sounds.

Don't bother trying to understand what they are. Just listen. Quietly. Silently. For one minute. And then open your eyes.

Note: Please do this practice before you read any further.

What Is Mindfulness?

Mindfulness means being aware of what is happening in your life, right at this moment.

In the above practice, when you focused on the sounds, you were trying to be mindful. However, your experience of the practice was probably somewhat like this: You closed your eyes and tried to focus. You heard a few sounds. You were able to notice them for a short while, but then you started thinking and forgot about listening. This is the typical experience of all those who try this practice.

When you try to focus on sounds, thoughts start to distract you. They take your attention away.

Even then, you have managed to learn something very useful about yourself, in just one minute!

And what was that?

You have learnt that even when you decide to listen to the sounds around you, your mind does not allow you to do so entirely. You get lost in thought even without realizing it. Your mind is not fully in your control!

You see, you have already started to understand your mind a bit. This is a great start.

Let's take this understanding a bit further. Where did your thoughts take you? If you revisit them, you will find that the thoughts took you to the past or to the future or there were some stories and comments about the present. All of this prevented you from actually experiencing the present.

Only when you were listening to the sounds were you actually connected to your life, as the sounds were all in the present moment.

Now to be a friend to yourself, it is very important that your mind is fully aware of what is happening with you now. For example, to be friendly with yourself, you need to know how you are feeling. It is, however, not possible to do that unless you are fully aware of your feelings in the present moment.

So training your mind to be present is the first step towards becoming friends with yourself.

2

MINDFULNESS: HOW IT ALL STARTED

'Mindfulness' is a popularly used word nowadays, but it is an ancient practice that originated in India.

Some of the concepts and practices that we will learn through the book have existed for thousands of years. They have been spoken of in old scriptures and texts.

In the last ten to twenty years, many scientific studies have been done on the brain. These studies have shown that mindfulness is very beneficial to us and helps us to live happier lives.

In telling you about mindfulness, I will give special attention to someone who explained the practice in detail about 2500 years ago. The name given to him was Siddhartha, and he is known to all of us as the Buddha or the Enlightened One.

THE STORY OF THE BUDDHA

Once, in a wealthy Shakya clan in India, was born a child named Siddhartha. He was very protected by his father, as his father wanted him to grow up and be a successful leader and king like himself. He thought that if he gave Siddhartha all the pleasures while keeping him unaware of any difficulties, then Siddhartha would get used to the pleasant life of the palace. He would naturally want to have these riches and pleasures all his life, eventually becoming a king.

But it was not to be so.

Siddhartha was a highly introspective and sensitive person. He had many questions on life and happiness, and he could not find those answers, even though he had all the pleasures one could hope for. He had everything, and yet, he felt something was missing. He felt that all the delights of the palace were not going to give him lasting happiness.

He realized that he would have clarity about life only when the deep layers of the mind were explored and understood.

And so, he left the palace and all worldly pleasures when he was twenty-nine. He left with no material possessions and went to the forest to spend time meditating—in pursuit of looking within and trying to know himself.

After many years of such practice, he became 'enlightened'.

An enlightened being is one who sees everything clearly and who finds answers to all the profound questions of life.

His years of meditation and questioning the fundamental nature of things helped him get perfect clarity about the nature of human beings, the truth of lasting happiness, and the reasons why people suffer. You could say he had become an expert psychologist or a mind expert.

He gave many teachings and tools to understand the mind. Some of the mindfulness concepts and practices included in this book are simplified versions of his teachings.

The Buddha's Core Teaching: The Four Noble Truths

Being a mind expert, the Buddha provided a simple explanation for why we remain unhappy. Before we get into his actual teaching, let us go over an example.

If you go to a doctor and say you have a stomach ache, what would the doctor do? They would try to understand the issue through these four steps:

*   Ask about the stomach pain to confirm that you do have it.
*   Try to understand what could have caused it.
*   Conclude and reach a solution.
*   Present the treatment, which might be prescribing medicines or a new diet plan.

The Buddha did precisely the same for our tendency to stay unhappy. He gave us four steps to understand and overcome our unhappiness. These are called the four Noble Truths.

These are the truths about human nature that apply to each and every one of us. These were applicable 2500 years ago when the Buddha lived, and they are still relevant now.

So here are the four Noble Truths:

*   There is *dukkha* (suffering or dissatisfaction).
*   There is a cause for the dukkha.

- There is a cure for the dukkha.
- There is a path (way of understanding and practising) to get out of this dukkha.

Let us start with the word 'dukkha' and understand it well. In ancient Indian literature, this word was found in both Sanskrit and Pali languages. *Du* is 'unpleasant' and *kha* is 'space'.

The Buddha says that there is a constant unpleasant space that we all experience. No matter how much we have, we are still dissatisfied. We keep feeling that something is missing.

Let us examine if this is true. Say, you have three friends among which one of them is not speaking to you, you'd feel the unpleasantness, right? You don't feel satisfied that the other two are on good terms with you. It is not enough.

Let's take other similar examples. If you score well in six subjects but not in two, you feel down. If your parents buy you a few things except that one particular thing that you particularly wanted, you feel dissatisfied and unhappy. The list is endless.

Hence, the first Noble Truth—'There is dukkha'—says that we constantly feel unhappy as though life is not good enough.

Even if things go well in life, we focus on the problems and spend our energy on finding solutions to them instead of living in the present and enjoying the things that are going well.

We believe that if we get that one thing that we want, we will become happy. If we get that one boy or girl's attention, we will be fine, or if our parents buy us that one game, we will be satisfied.

But the Buddha encourages us to reflect: is that so?

Even if we do get something, we become satisfied only for a short while. Soon, we have another problem that we worry about or another thing that we want. We become dissatisfied and miserable again pretty quickly.

So, the first step in knowing ourselves well is recognizing that we have dukkha or a tendency to always stay dissatisfied—just like everyone else. Only if we acknowledge or recognize our dukkha can we learn how to get over it.

EXERCISE: LET US REFLECT ON DUKKHA

Answer the questions below thoughtfully and honestly. These questions will help you understand your mind better. You can revisit them whenever needed. Use this space to write your thoughts.

1. What is it that you find yourself longing for or thinking too much about?

   _____

   _____

2. How do you feel when you cannot get the thing you want or when the problem you are thinking about does not get resolved?

   _____

   _____

3. Can you list one or two examples about how overthinking or worrying about something did not let you be happy or

enjoy something in the present? For instance, I can think of a situation where I did not know how to tell my friend she was annoying me and I kept thinking about how she was upsetting me instead of enjoying the party we were at. Can you think of something like this that happened to you?

_____

_____

4. Name one thing that you wanted in the past, which you got after some time. I am sure you were happy to get it. But do you remember for how long you stayed happy before you wanted something else and you were dissatisfied again?

_____

_____

Let us reflect on these questions. Take it slow. Read your answers again if you need to.

You can see for yourself that you get dissatisfied often. You want to get everything you want. You want all of life's problems to go away. But since that is simply not possible, you are stuck in this cycle of being satisfied for some time and then again becoming dissatisfied. Can this ever be a happy way to live?

This is what the Buddha meant when he spoke of dukkha.

Is There Any Good News?

The idea that we are so often dissatisfied is upsetting! However, I promise there is only good news and better news from here on.

The most encouraging is the third Noble Truth. It says that the cycle of dukkha and dissatisfaction can end, and that there is a possibility of living a happy life if we are willing to put in effort to gradually change our mindset so as to try and understand afresh what true happiness really is.

The Buddha said that we all have a seed of wisdom within us. This seed is also called the 'Buddha nature' or the 'nature of wise understanding'. He said we all have a wise inner nature that knows how to live happily.

Just like a seed needs regular water to grow into a plant, this source of wisdom that is deep inside us needs watering and attention. When we practise being mindful and staying connected to the reality of our lives, we are giving this seed the right conditions to flourish and grow. When we get caught up in unwise thoughts, this seed does not get the nourishment it needs.

Let us start watering this seed right away by doing some meditation.

What Is Meditation?

Meditation is a practice done with complete focus. Most of the practices in this book will be those of mindfulness meditation. This means we will meditate keeping our attention fully focused on the present.

Earlier, we practised listening to sounds mindfully for just a minute. We did that without understanding why we were doing it. But now we know that paying attention to sounds in the present moment is a way of connecting to ourselves, to our inner wisdom, and our Buddha nature.

So let us practise meditating on sounds now.

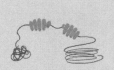

PRACTICE: MEDITATION WITH SOUNDS

When meditating on sounds, it is important to remember that we are not trying to identify the sounds or understand where they are coming from. We are just learning to train our minds to *stay* with the sounds in the present.

We are simply listening quietly. By this simple act of paying attention to sounds, we can train our minds to become peaceful.

Here is a contemplative poem for your inspiration. Read it slowly. Then you can start your practice.

TO ALL SOUNDS

As I mindfully listen, I start to hear
The sound of the cat that searches for food,
The birds before sunset that come home to roost,
The waves of the sea and the sounds of the stream,
My mom's call for food and the doorbell's chime.
I hear the car's loud horn,

The soft groan of my grandpa's pain.
I hear, I accept, I listen in silent meditation
To all sounds, again and again.

After reading this verse, set a stopwatch or timer for five minutes. Close your eyes, relax and start listening to the sounds around you.

Which sounds feel near to you? Spend some time listening to these sounds. Which sounds are far away from you? Spend some time on them too.

Remember, you are simply listening to all the sounds. You are accepting both pleasant and unpleasant sounds. This is meditating on sounds. This is also a beautiful way to experience the world. Keep your eyes closed and continue until your alarm rings.

3

PLEASURE VS HAPPINESS: CHOOSING WISELY

Which Gift Will You Choose?

Imagine a scenario where I give you two gift boxes: one that looks very pretty and is decorated beautifully, and the other that looks simple and is wrapped in just brown paper. I then ask you to select one. Which one would you choose?

Most probably, the pretty one.

However, when you open the pretty gift box, you find something that makes you upset. Then I ask you to open the other gift too. In the simply wrapped box, you find something beautiful, precious and invaluable.

Which gift do you now want?

Naturally, the second one. The reason is, now you know which one holds the real gift.

Pleasure and happiness are like that. Pleasure is an upsetting gift in a pretty box. We keep choosing it because it looks attractive. But in the long run, it makes us upset and unhappy. We will understand more about it soon.

Happiness is a precious gift in a simple box. We don't choose it because it doesn't look appealing at the outset. But when we really experience it, we realize its worth.

Everyone wants to be happy. Parents, children, teenagers and elderly people too. But all of us make the same error.

We choose the wrong gift box. We confuse pleasure with happiness.

We can only make the right choice if we understand the difference between the two. Let's focus on understanding pleasure first.

What Is Pleasure?

Let's take an example.

You are really craving ice cream and you want to eat it soon. Now two things can happen:

1. You get to eat the ice cream of your choice.
2. You do not get the ice cream. Maybe your parents refuse to let you go out, or the shop is closed or for some reason, you just don't get to eat it.

Now let us see what happens in each scenario.

In scenario one, where you get the ice cream, you feel pleased and satisfied for some time. The first few spoonfuls are delicious, but then you may become a little less excited.

In scenario two, where you do not get ice cream, you feel upset. Maybe you get angry at your parents for not letting you go out or you get sulky that the shop is closed. Basically, you lose your peace of mind for a while.

So, what has really happened is this: getting the ice cream has satisfied you but only for a short time; not getting it has made you upset immediately.

Let us take another example so that you understand better. This time, let us use a not-so-obvious example.

You have fared better than usual in the recent tests. You worked hard this time. You want your parents to acknowledge that and say something that makes you feel good.

Again, two scenarios are possible:

1. Your parents recognize your hard work and praise you. Maybe they take you out for dinner or even buy you something you wanted.
2. Your parents don't acknowledge that your results are because of your hard work. Instead, maybe they say you got lucky in these tests or that the test was too easy. Or perhaps they don't say much at all. They just don't react.

Here, again, as in the previous example, you feel good only when you get what you want. In this case, it is the appreciation from your parents. When you don't get what you want or expect, you feel discouraged and unhappy.

Both the above examples are of seeking pleasure.

Whether you are craving ice cream or your parents' attention and appreciation, you are only feeling good if you get what you want and feeling low when you don't.

Pleasure has the following common characteristics:

- **In pleasure, feeling good is conditional**: This means that you feel good depending on conditions outside you. Both getting ice cream and attention from your parents are external factors. If the conditions are in your favour, you feel good. If not, you feel upset.
- **Getting pleasure is often out of your control**: What you *want* is in your control, but what you *get* is not in your control. For example, the ice cream shop being closed is not something you have any control over. Your parents appreciating you or not is also not in your control.

- **Pleasure is temporary:** This means that even if you get what you want, you feel pleased only for a short while. After some time, the good feeling ends and you crave something else. If you eat ice cream once, you are not happy for life; you will want ice cream again. Or maybe, because you got ice cream and ate it, you will now forget about it and want something else. So, even if one desire is satisfied, it is not enough.
- **Chasing pleasure leads to pain and unhappiness:** When you want something that you believe will make you feel good but you don't get it, you become outrightly unhappy. If you don't get the ice cream when you want it, it makes you upset. When your parents don't acknowledge your hard work, you feel low.

Let's analyse this trap of pleasure. When you get what you want, the good feeling ends pretty quickly and when you don't get what you want, you are unhappy immediately.

Doesn't sound like real happiness, does it? Yet we pursue pleasure all the time! Why?

Because it is exciting and there is a rush of a positive feeling when we get something we want. We like that rush and assume that this is happiness. We mistakenly believe that if we keep deriving more and more pleasure, we will become happy forever. Pleasure looks attractive, like the delicious-looking ice cream. It feels pleasant, like the warm feeling brought on by your parents appreciating you. It is like the pretty decorated gift box.

But inside the gift box, there is the not-so-pleasant side of pleasure, which we don't see.

Pleasure has a short life. It ends pretty quickly.

When it goes away, it leaves us feeling empty, as though we are missing something. It leaves us craving and wanting more. So, what do we do? We restlessly start searching for another thing, situation or person to give us that pleasure, and this goes on and on.

This constant seeking of pleasure is what the Buddha called as the cycle of dukkha or the cycle of dissatisfaction.

Obviously, we do not get all that we want. Over time, we only get exhausted from running after things, wanting more in life, and become more and more unhappy.

It is so ironic, right? We are trying to find happiness. Instead, we are unknowingly moving towards unhappiness.

What Is Happiness?

A spiritual teacher from Maharashtra, Nisargadatta Maharaj said, 'Instead of searching for what you do not have, find out what it is that you have never lost.'

He is asking us to look within instead of searching outside for happiness. Happiness is within us all the time. It is our natural state of being. But we have to discover it.

A good analogy is water that is present underneath the ground. We don't realize it exists because we cannot see it. But if we put in effort and dig a well, we can find enough water to support an entire village for years.

The water was always there. But to discover it, some effort was needed. Similarly, happiness is within us, but we have to find a way to it.

Happiness is very different from pleasure. It is a lasting state of feeling at ease, at rest and at peace. It is the simple-looking box with a precious gift.

Happiness can be discovered when you connect to the present moment and accept it. Here is a simple practice that will connect you to the ease and peace within you, right now.

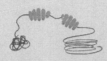

PRACTICE: RECOGNIZING HAPPINESS

Close your eyes for a minute. Try not to move or to want anything. Any thoughts that come to you can just pass by. Don't give them any importance. When you don't give any importance to thoughts, you may notice that thoughts simply come and go, and that you can be at rest with the quiet space inside you.

Can you stay with this quiet space? Can you try to enjoy it a little or at least accept it and rest there? This place of peace and OK-ness is happiness. It is there within you always. Your practice is to learn to be with it and enjoy it.

When you can rest with yourself in this manner, you realize you need not depend on pleasure to make you feel good. When you want ice cream, you realize you may or may not get it. The situation is not fully in your control. So you do not let your joy *depend* upon it. You apply your understanding of mindfulness and remain peaceful even if you do not get the ice cream.

When you do get the ice cream, you pay full attention to eating it and enjoy it mindfully. This way, you become relaxed and happy because you know life is not about getting everything you *want* but enjoying what you *have*. You become a contented person.

However, remember that knowing this is not enough. As you might forget this soon, you have to practise this way of being.

Here is another short practice to help you connect with the inner state of relaxation and happiness. You can do both this practice and the one above any time during the day, even if you just have one minute.

PRACTICE: BREATHING HAPPINESS

Close your eyes and focus on your breath. As you breathe in, mentally say, 'Breathing in, I turn inwards.'

Now, breathing out, tell yourself, 'Breathing out, I feel happy.'

Do this for at least five breaths.

When you say, 'Breathing in, I turn inwards,' try and focus your attention on your chest area. When you say, 'Breathing out, I feel happy,' try and notice the rest and relaxation that comes over you when you exhale.

Now, open your eyes and see how you feel.

You can do this practice whenever you feel like taking a pause in your day.

The Difference between Pleasure and Happiness

Here is a quick and easy way to distinguish between pleasure and happiness so you don't confuse the two:

PLEASURE	HAPPINESS
• It is exciting and stimulating.	• It is peaceful and restful.
• There are ups and downs.	• There is a general OK-ness and mostly calm feeling.
• The highs and exciting times are temporary. They disappear after some time.	• The joyful and peaceful feeling is lasting.

• When we don't have excitement, we can become irritable, bored, low, snappy and even depressed.	• There is no concept of ups and downs. We are not addicted to highs and excitement. So, we also don't feel irritated and low when there is less excitement.

- We keep searching for more pleasure because we cannot bear not having a high, and this constant search can tire us.

- We can be happy in the present, in whatever is there in our life right now, so we don't search for much and therefore, stay energized.

THE STORY OF JETSUNMA TENZIN PALMO

Here is a story about an extraordinary lady who spent twelve years in a cave by herself in the Himalayas.

She was a British person who came to India and adopted the Tibetan Buddhist tradition. She is now respectfully known as Jetsunma Tenzin Palmo and is a nun and a teacher in the same tradition.

One crucial part of Buddhist teachings is that people need to spend time getting to know themselves. They can do this in a quiet retreat, in a monastery, or in a space where they can be by themselves and completely silent.

Jetsunma chose to spend time by herself in a cave. In her biography *Cave in the Snow*, she describes her time spent there in detail.

Isn't this intriguing? Why did she choose to spend so many years in a cave instead of enjoying the pleasures of life?

Like all of us, she could have chosen to watch movies, TV, hang out with friends and party. Instead, why did she choose such a solitary and difficult life?

This is what I have understood from following her teachings for years: She clearly knew that pleasure wasn't really worth seeking. That true happiness was to be found within, in understanding the true nature of the self.

She wanted to understand why and how the mind keeps moving from one distraction to another, always restless. She did this by meditating in complete silence.

4

TO UNDERSTAND IS TO LOVE

We can be true friends with ourselves and love ourselves only when we understand and accept ourselves. In this chapter, we will try to spend some time doing just that.

Unfortunately, most of us have been made to feel that we need to be 'special' and 'better than others' to be good. We run races trying to win, we compete in class trying to come first, we try to impress people and create a good image in their minds about us.

We are happy with who we are only when others say we are good. We look for their approval. We doubt ourselves and become upset when people criticize or judge us.

Let us take a moment here and ask ourselves this simple question: In a school, in a class of twenty students, can anybody be better than everybody else at everything? It is impossible!

All students have different skills and aptitudes. Some are better at one skill and have certain qualities. Others are better at other skills and possess different qualities. And yet, so many of us are trying to be the best and to get the attention and praise of others to feel good.

When we keep striving to be better than others all the time, we do not accept ourselves for who we are. This is a recipe for a very unhappy life, full of insecurity. And we are definitely not being friendly towards ourselves.

So how can you change this way of being? To start with, you can make a change by repeatedly reminding yourself of the truth. But what is this truth?

You are already special . . . and so is everyone else!

This statement is the entire truth because everyone is made special, and you need to remind yourself of it regularly.

Here is a quick activity that will help you remember this every day.

EXERCISE: REMEMBERING THE TRUTH

On a piece of paper, write this down: 'I am special. So is everyone else'.

Now stick this sheet on your mirror, cupboard or bathroom. Put it in a place where you see it often. Look at it every day and remind yourself that this is the truth.

The thought here is that you are not more or less special than anyone else. Everyone is *differently* special. Everyone has unique gifts. Some people have 'gifts' that are easily seen by the world. They may be good-looking, excellent at sports or studies, great singers, or have a great sense of fashion.

Others may have gifts that are not easily seen. They may be helpful and kind, fantastic at mental calculation, at keeping

their cupboard neat and organized, or be very creative in their way of thinking.

Whether or not your gifts are seen and appreciated by others, they are there. The problem arises when you do not realize that you are special, you spend too much time and energy trying to be better than others instead of enjoying your own gifts.

Here is the story of Ananya that will make this idea clearer.

How We Lose Friendship with Ourselves

Ananya was fifteen years old. She had few friends in school. She often compared herself with other, more popular classmates, and felt that she just wasn't good enough. She especially compared herself with Tamara, who was the most popular girl in class. Most of the time, she felt jealous when Tamara was praised.

Tamara was the teacher's favourite and had many friends. Everyone wanted to be in Tamara's company. Ananya felt no one cared whether she existed or not.

Now let us analyse this situation. Ananya felt no one cared for her because she did not match up to Tamara's popularity. She felt she was just not good enough.

Is that the truth though? Did no one care for Ananya? Was she not good enough? The truth often has more layers than we recognize.

Here are some aspects of Ananya's reality that she did not give importance to:

Ananya had two good friends. Even though she was not as popular as Tamara, her friends really liked her and were close to her.

However, Ananya could not appreciate the gift of her two friends because her mind was preoccupied with thoughts about Tamara's popularity. She underestimated the joy of having good friends and took their presence in her life for granted.

Ananya sang well and enjoyed singing. But she did not consider it to be a gift at all. She only ever sang in the bathroom or when alone.

She was also a kind-hearted person and was sensitive towards other people's feelings. She tried not to hurt people. But again, she did not count this as a gift, since others did not express appreciation for this quality in her.

This is how Ananya could not appreciate the gifts she had. She could not enjoy them. She could not accept herself for who she really was. Instead, as Tamara became more popular, she became more miserable.

If you were Ananya's friend, wouldn't you remind her of how special she really was? Wouldn't you ask her to pay more attention to what she already had and not focus too much on Tamara?

We have to learn to do the same with ourselves.

Like Ananya, we often judge ourselves based on how others see us. We think that only those gifts that bring praise or attention from others matter, and that other gifts don't.

Slowly, we stop liking ourselves. Since we are not getting as much attention as we want, we believe we are not good enough. We disregard our gifts, and gradually, we lose friendship with ourselves.

Now here is what you need to remember when this happens to you and when you don't feel good enough: nature does not think like you!

Nature has created you to be exactly as you are.

Just like everything in nature is essential and much needed—every leaf and flower, every butterfly and beetle, every mosquito—you are too. Nature does not think, 'Oh, I like this bee more than that flower.' Or 'I prefer this sweet-smelling rose to that yellow blade of grass.'

Nature does not compare and choose. Nature also does not create anything that is not needed. Nature has made you exactly as you are and everyone else exactly as they are because that is how we all need to be.

Nature has created lemons, mangoes as well as the bitter neem leaf. Why did it not make everything sweet like a mango? Because nature is very intelligent. It knows that all different qualities are needed for the world to exist. Everything cannot be like everything else. Every single plant, animal, insect and person is unique.

We all are equally important parts of this whole world. So there is really no point in comparing ourselves with each other.

Instead, enjoy your life and your gifts fully. If you are good at the piano, enjoy playing it. If you are not so good at maths, try figuring it out. It is your way of saying thank you to nature for whatever it has given to you.

Thank nature for your strengths but also for your weaknesses, because both make you who you are!

Here is a small exercise to get you started on the path of appreciating your gifts and being friends with yourself.

EXERCISE: CELEBRATING THE GOOD IN YOU

In this exercise, you need to list all the good things about yourself. It is often difficult to see what is good in us, so anything that you like about yourself must be put down here.

You don't have to judge your abilities and strengths by what anyone else thinks. Maybe you have a loving heart. Or you are a good friend. Or you are strong and well built. Maybe you study well or are good at dancing. Perhaps you care for your parents or feed stray cats. All these are gifts.

So let's do this step by step.

Step 1: Write down five things you like about yourself.
(For example, here is what I would pick as one of the gifts I like about myself: I am enthusiastic).

1. _____

2. _____

3. _____

4. _____

5. _____

Step 2: Now take each of the above points you have written and complete the following sentences.

(For example, mine would be: I appreciate you for being enthusiastic.)

1. I appreciate you for _____.
2. I appreciate you for _____.
3. I appreciate you for _____.
4. I appreciate you for _____.
5. I appreciate you for _____.

Step 3: Now visualize yourself sitting in a relaxed way, peacefully. Look at your imagined image for a few seconds. Then mentally say to your image each of the sentences in step 2. Smile at your image after each sentence.

For example, if your gift is being a helpful person, then imagine yourself sitting in front of you and say to yourself, 'I appreciate you for being a helpful person.' Repeat each sentence as many times as you feel like saying it or until you feel good about saying it.

After this exercise, notice how you are feeling.

*   Were you able to wholeheartedly appreciate yourself for your gifts?
*   Did you feel good about yourself?

Even if you did not, this is only the beginning. You are just getting started. You may not yet be great friends with yourself, but you have definitely taken a step on that path.

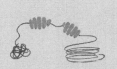

PRACTICE: APPRECIATE YOURSELF EVERY DAY

Every day, find one thing to appreciate about yourself. Try to notice one quality, deed or thought that you like about you. Maybe you were helpful or kind, answered a question in class, or made a painting. It does not matter what it is. Simply find something to appreciate yourself for every day.

5

GENTLE EFFORT IS KEY

When you want to learn to play the piano or the guitar, you need to practise regularly. Similarly, when trying to understand yourself, you need to put in some effort consistently. You need to make a few ideas and practices a part of your daily life.

The important thing, though, is to keep the effort very gentle in nature. If your goal is to become happy and peaceful, the nature of your effort must also be kind and peaceful.

There are some ways that I have suggested here that will help you gently include the ideas and practices into your life.

1. Spend silent time with yourself

Take out some time every day to just be with yourself.

Keep your phone, tablet and all other distractions aside. Let your family members know you are going to be silent and by yourself for some time.

It could just be two or five minutes to start with. When you start enjoying this silent time, you can extend it for a few minutes more.

Sit somewhere peacefully and simply observe what you see and what you hear. Or you can also just focus on your breathing.

Adding silent times to your day is a great way to learn to be your own friend. When you learn to sit silently, enjoying your breath, you easily acquire the art of staying happy.

If you find staying silent with nothing to do difficult, you can use the practice below to help you stay mindful during the silent time.

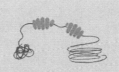

VISUALIZATION PRACTICE: THE SILENT ISLAND

Imagine you are on an island. A beautiful island. Lush green. A gentle breeze. Blue waves of water. The birds are chirping.

Take some time to create this visual in your mind. Enjoy being here. This island is only for you, and it can be as you like. You are here by yourself, but you don't feel alone. Because you are your own friend. You sit by a sandy beach on this island and decide: 'I will rest here for a few minutes and just enjoy being with myself.'

After imagining this, start your practice with a gentle smile. Be glad you took time out for yourself. You take time out for so many things, but now you have found time to just be with you.

Your companion here can be your breath. It is always there, nourishing you, keeping you alive, whether you pay attention to it or not. Bring your attention to your breath. Breathe in slowly at first. Stay aware of the entire breath as it goes in. Notice where you feel it in your nostrils. Where else can you feel it? Maybe in your throat or in the rising of your chest or belly. Notice it. Then stay mindful of it as it leaves your body.

Great! You have started resting and getting comfortable with yourself.

Now do this for ten breaths. Stay fully aware of each inhalation and exhalation. Give it all your attention.

After ten such breaths, gently open your eyes.

This island is now yours. It is always with you. You can return to it whenever you want to be with yourself.

2. Pay attention to your life

'Pay attention!' How many times have you heard that from your parents and teachers? I certainly did too many times!

It is kind of funny that I should be talking to you about attention, since I was such an inattentive and distracted child in school. My teachers would regularly complain to my parents about how distracted I was.

They were quite right. I remember looking out of the classroom window and daydreaming a lot, to get over the boredom of being in class.

But here I am telling you the opposite. I am sharing with you the benefit of paying attention. This is because after I started to pay attention to life mindfully, I started feeling so much more free and joyful. I believe paying attention to the present moment is crucial to becoming happy.

And I am not talking of only paying attention in class. Paying attention to everything is vital: to eating, brushing, walking, bathing, watering the plants, doing homework.

Here is a lovely story about a wise elder from a village that points to this.

THE WISE ELDER

A long time ago, there was an elder living in a village who was known to be very wise and happy.

A man once went to him and asked, 'What makes you so wise, respected sir?'

To this, the elder responded, 'When I eat, I only eat; when I sleep, I simply sleep; when I talk to someone, I fully dedicate myself to doing just that.'

'But I can do that too without being wise,' the man answered.

'I don't think so,' the wise elder said. 'When you eat, you are thinking about the problems you had throughout the day. While you are talking with me, you are thinking about what to ask me or what to answer before I am done talking.'

Then he confided, 'The secret is to be mindful of what we are doing in the present moment. Then we can enjoy every minute of the miracle that is life.'

Every day is made up of small moments. There are so many moments that you can enjoy only if you notice and pay attention to them.

You start your morning by brushing your teeth. But have you ever paid attention to brushing your teeth? Have you ever tried to just brush your teeth and think of nothing else?

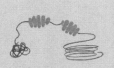

PRACTICE: BEING FULLY AWARE

The next time you brush your teeth, try to stay in the present. This means, try to brush your teeth by paying attention to the action of brushing. Try and know when your hands move, which tooth is being cleaned and how you are doing it. You brush your teeth every day, but rarely do you do it mindfully, with full awareness.

Similarly, you can enjoy so many things throughout the day, by paying attention to them.

You take a bath in the morning, but usually, you'd be thinking about something else and bathing without really experiencing it. Try to enjoy the water running down your body. The warm water makes you feel fresh and energetic. Enjoy the fragrance of the soap. Feel the towel on your skin. When you finish your bath, you will feel relaxed because you paid attention to bathing.

When you eat your breakfast, you can try to enjoy what you are eating. Pay attention to every morsel of food. Enjoy its taste.

Perhaps you travel to school by foot, or the school bus or a car. You can pay attention to what you see around you, like people rushing to work or selling or buying items from stores. You realize that when you are seeing all this and not thinking, you are resting and enjoying.

Initially, you may not find any sense in being in the present. You may even find it boring. But slowly, it will start to make you feel peaceful and rested as you begin to enjoy simple daily activities.

3. Say a thank you to nature: practise gratitude

Gratitude is the practice of saying a thank you to nature, when we experience something comforting and pleasant.

When you receive a gift from someone, you naturally show gratitude. You are happy, and you thank the person who gave you the present. However, our days are full of small gifts that we don't notice and take for granted.

We go to play a sport we like and really enjoy it. Or we return home from a long walk and have a refreshing drink of water. These are also enjoyable feelings that we can thank nature for.

Perhaps you may think, 'Yeah, whatever! Why should I be so thankful about a glass of water or a sport? I drink water all the time or I play the sport every day.'

This is what your mind is saying. Our minds are not tuned in to gratitude. Our minds are not oriented to noticing the positives in our life.

It's not just your mind. Everyone's mind is like that! In fact, our minds are more used to focusing on the negative or difficult situations rather than being grateful for the positive ones.

For instance, when the weather is nice and cool, we don't feel very thankful for such good weather. But when it is hot, or the sun is very sharp, we are quick to complain.

We continue to notice the things that aren't going well. We complain often. 'This is boring!', 'She is mean!', 'It is hot!', 'This is not enough!', 'The food is not tasty!' and so on.

Since we pay more attention to unpleasant things around us, they occupy quite a bit of our mind. We end up paying less attention to the joyful situations and miss out on the opportunity to enjoy them. With time, we become less happy.

Let's take an example to see how this happens.

Rahul's twelfth birthday was close. His parents wanted to make it memorable for him. They knew he wanted a branded football, sports shoes and a video game. To surprise him, his parents had bought all three. They also decided to hold two different parties: one for family and one for friends.

Rahul then asked them for a solar robot construction kit for his birthday. His parents had, however, already bought three presents. Since this kit was also quite expensive, they decided they would buy it the next time.

On his birthday, his parents gave him the gifts they had bought. What do you think his reaction was? He opened all three, pulled a face and said, 'Oh no! You did not get the robot kit. I really wanted that!'

Let's analyse what is actually happening with Rahul. He is in the middle of his birthday party with friends. He has three presents, all of which he has wanted at some point. He is feeling no gratitude for his gifts or for the party, because his mind is preoccupied with the one present he did not get.

Rahul is not a spoilt or ungrateful person. He is just like most of us. He is focusing on what is missing so much that he is letting all the good stuff pass him by.

Like Rahul, we also let so many beautiful moments in our lives pass by without enjoying them because we do not have exactly what we want.

So, how can we change this tendency? How can we learn to enjoy what we have?

Firstly, by shifting our attention away from thinking about what is missing and what is not good enough, and actively paying attention to what is going well.

Secondly, when we do notice the good stuff, saying a thank you to nature for it. It could be something very small. You could feel happy about a puppy you saw on your way to school and feel grateful for it. Or for a sweet that your friend offered you today. Or some food that you found tasty.

Remember, it is not a forced thank you for something you do not feel. When you are being mindful, you are making friends with who you are. There is no space for dishonesty. Even if you cannot think of anything to be grateful for, it's okay. Look out for these small comforting and happy moments the next day.

Like everything else, this too is a practice, a practice of training your mind to recognize that good things are happening all the time. You are training the mind by focusing on the positives and again and again bringing to mind what is going well in life. It is not just a one-time exercise. You need to do this every day, every time something goes well so that your mind gets habituated to focusing on the positives.

Come, let us begin this beautiful gratitude practice right away.

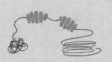

PRACTICE: GRATITUDE AS A WAY OF LIFE

In this practice, we will consciously try to remember the good around us and then appreciate it by feeling thankful for it.

Close your eyes and take three deep breaths, all the while being mindful of your breathing. It will create some space in your mind and help you to think clearly.

Then bring to mind the things that you are glad about. It could be something that happened today or something that is a part of your life. It could also be someone in your life like your parents, siblings, grandparents, a pet or a friend.

Or perhaps you enjoy playing an instrument or a sport. Or going to the park and playing in the evenings makes you happy. Or you really like a teacher in school.

> Whatever this person or activity or thing is that makes you happy, take a moment to imagine it. See a picture in your mind's eye about it. Thank life for giving it to you.
> Smile gently, and then open your eyes.

See, such a simple practice. And yet so powerful because it has the potential to change the tendency of the mind to lean towards negative thinking.

I sometimes say thank you for birdsong or a flower or for the breeze. But you know what, we all have lots and lots to say thank you for. We have eyes, ears, taste buds, arms and legs. We can see, hear, feel and do such beautiful things. We can always say thank you for these!

Sometimes, we allow one negative event to outweigh the positives of a day. But there are almost always good moments, even on days that are challenging.

So, let us make a decision to practise gratitude every day. A good time to do this is at night, just before sleeping. Just before you go to sleep, take a moment to say 'thank you' for all the good things in your life today. This is the simplest gratitude practice.

To start you on this practice, notice one pleasant event every day for the next week and write a small note about how it made you feel. (You can use the reflection space at the end of this section to jot down your notes.)

Here are some examples of what your entry could look like:

I saw a cute puppy on the road to school today. Seeing it made me feel happy. Thank you for that puppy.

Today, my friend shared her classwork notes with me. I was delighted that she was kind to me and that she liked me. Thank you for my friend's kindness.

That is all it takes. One positive, happy situation that you are thankful for every day. You simply write it down. Then it can become a daily habit and help you connect with your inner joyfulness.

4. Understand that everything changes

Once you come to the understanding that things change, it can make you feel free and light. Let us understand our relationship with change.

Let us say you are having a great time at your friend's place, but it is now time to go back home. You are not ready to return yet. You want to stay a bit longer. You ask your mom if you could stay for another hour. Your mom refuses and asks you to come home right away. You feel down and upset because you have to leave despite wanting to stay.

Now let's introspect a bit. What is really upsetting you? You probably think that you are upset because your mom did not allow you to stay longer. But let us think this through.

When you decided to go to your friend's place, did you know it was going to be for a short time? Yes, of course, you did. Did you know that you will have to return home? Yes, you did! Then why is actually doing so upsetting you so much? Because you are not ready for the good time you are having to get over. You don't want it to change.

Even though we know things do change and everything is impermanent, we do not easily accept change in day-to-day life. We do not want things to change when they are going well. Change makes us uneasy.

But things change whether we want them to or not. In fact, everything is constantly changing. That is the way of life—and it is good too.

When you get hurt, you feel immense pain for some time. Then slowly, you heal and the pain reduces. This is also change. If things were not to change, you wouldn't get better.

If we understand change and accept it as a part of life, we can become peaceful and happy. When things are good, we will enjoy them fully, knowing that they will change. When life is difficult, we will stay patient, knowing that too will change. And that is such a sensible and settled way of being.

Here is a lovely story that explains a wise way to look at change and impermanence.

THIS TOO SHALL PASS

A rich man died, leaving two sons behind. They decided to separate, dividing all the properties between themselves equally.

After all the matters relating to the properties were settled, the two brothers came across a small packet that was carefully hidden by their father. The packet contained two rings: one was an expensive diamond ring, and the other was an ordinary silver ring that didn't cost a lot.

Seeing the diamond ring, the elder brother developed greed and desired the ring for himself. He explained to the younger brother, 'This packet is obviously a family heirloom and not part of the joint family property. Our father probably wanted the diamond ring to be passed down from generation to generation and stay within the family. Being the elder brother, I will take the diamond ring. You had better take the silver one.'

The younger brother smiled and agreed. He understood why his father had preserved the expensive diamond ring, but he was curious about why he had kept the silver ring, which had very little value. He took the ring and examined it. On the ring were written the words 'This too shall pass'.

The younger brother mused aloud, 'Oh, this was my father's motto: This too shall pass.' He then wore the ring on his finger.

Time passed. Both brothers went through the ups and downs of life. The elder brother would get delighted when spring came, for his farms would do well and he would become prosperous. Every spring, he used to feel that everything would be better now. But when spring would pass and winter would arrive, his farms would not do well, and he would become worried, depressed and unhappy.

The younger brother enjoyed the spring when it came. But he always remembered his father's motto: 'This too shall pass'. He did not become attached to the good times but enjoyed them while they lasted. He knew that spring would go. And when it did, he said to himself, 'It was definitely going to pass, and now it has gone. So what?'

Similarly, when winter approached and circumstances became difficult, he did not become agitated and unhappy but remembered, *This too shall pass*. He knew the tough times would also not last.

Thus, he could preserve his sense of balance through all the ups and downs of life and live happily.

Let's take inspiration from this story and do a practice to recognize change and impermanence.

PRACTICE: RECOGNIZE CHANGE AND IMPERMANENCE

As you read this, everything around and inside you is continuously changing. You may, however, not be aware of it. So come, let us become more aware of change and impermanence, one step at a time.

- Start by looking around you. Notice what is changing around you at this moment. Is the clock ticking away?

That is change. What do you see outside the window? Cars moving? Birds flying? People walking? See all of that as change. When a bird flies or a car moves, it is in a different place every minute than it was in the previous. There is continuous change.

- Now, do the same with sounds. What do you hear? Are the sounds changing? Even if you hear the ticking of a clock, every tick is a new tick. Do you hear birds chirping? Sounds of traffic? Television? Your family members speaking to each other? All sounds are constantly changing.

   Close your eyes for a few minutes and experience the changing sounds. Then you can open them and read further.

- Now, bring your attention to what is changing in your body. Just as everything is changing outside, everything within you is also in the process of continuous change. Your heart is beating. Fresh blood is getting pumped into your body with each beat. Your breath is changing. With every breath, you breathe in new air. Even though you cannot feel it, your organs are constantly working and changing, food is getting digested, kidneys are filtering water, all cells are changing.

   Close your eyes and try to notice this constant change inside you. Notice how every breath is changing. Just pay attention to its movement inside your body. After noticing a few breaths, open your eyes.

- Your mind is also changing. Your thoughts are continuously changing. Notice your thoughts for a few minutes. Close your eyes and experience them. Thoughts, ideas and feelings come and go. Try to be silent for some time and you will notice this. After a few minutes, open your eyes.

This practice will help you to see how change is just everywhere and also understand that you cannot control this change. Conditions outside you are out of your control. But it is the same with the conditions within. You cannot decide how much or when your heart should beat. Or how your digestion should take place. It is completely out of your control.

This practice, therefore, teaches you to let go of trying to control things. It teaches you to live peacefully with the ever-changing nature of life and maybe to even appreciate it.

5. Be kind to yourself and others

Being kind to yourself means being friendly towards yourself when you go through a challenging time. Sometimes, you feel hurt, sad, angry or unhappy. You can be kind to yourself by understanding that it is okay to feel this.

You can say, 'I am feeling down. I need my own care and support. I will take care of myself.' Just as we care about our friends or family members when they are feeling low, we can care for ourselves too.

When we learn to care for ourselves, we also become kind to others because we begin to understand that they too go through sadness and loneliness just like we do.

As you read the sections ahead on making friends with your mind and making friends with your feelings, you will understand how to practise kindness with yourself and others better. (Also refer to the metta practice on page 89.)

But for now, just understand that it is okay to feel any difficult feelings and to remain kind to yourself.

6. Put your trust in nature

As we have seen, we are so often out of control. We feel so overwhelmed and uneasy when this happens. In these times, we forget that we are created by nature, which is larger than us and much more intelligent. It has created the whole universe, including us, and is keeping everything in harmony.

Think of nature as a painter with a vast canvas, a canvas that spans galaxies. We are merely a tiny dot on this canvas. We cannot understand the entire painting.

We don't know why we are put in a particular position or situation or given specific qualities. But the painter knows what the big picture needs to look like. So, we need to put our trust in the painter and believe it knows best.

When times are difficult and we find no solutions to our problems, we can be patient, trusting nature to do what is right. We can surrender to nature, believing its superlative or brilliant intelligence knows better.

There is a beautiful *doha* or couplet by Kabir, about this kind of patience. This doha is among my favourites.

Dheere dheere re mana, dheere sab kuchh hoye,
Mali seenche sau ghada, rut aaye phal hoye.

This means:

O my mind, be patient. In good time, all shall unfold.
Even if a gardener waters a tree with a hundred pots of
water, the tree will only bear fruit when the season is right.

In this doha, Kabir is saying that even if the gardener works very hard to get fruit early, it will not happen until the right season for the fruit arrives. The gardener needs to patiently wait for the right time.

This is Kabir's message to us. Be patient, wait for the right time and leave things in nature's capable hands. This does not mean that we stop putting in effort. It simply means we try our best, but then leave the final result to nature.

For example, let us say you play the flute and have a performance to give. You can practise seriously and play the flute to the best of your ability, but you shouldn't worry too much about the result of your performance. Leave that to life, to nature.

This is the idea of surrender, of letting go of control and trusting nature.

Here is a contemplative poem I have written for you that you can use to further understand the concept of surrender. There are such contemplative poems throughout the book. They are written to help you reflect on specific ideas. This poem about a leaf will help you develop trust, patience and surrender, even when things are difficult.

THE LEAF

I look at a leaf, a tiny sprout,
Almost pink, yet not green.

Tender, breakable, but fearless.
I see it grow.
I see nature give it water and sunlight.
In time, it is ripe and green,
It enjoys its shine and youth.
It rustles in the strong breeze,
And at times, the birds peck at it.
But often, it is just still and silent.

As days go by, it turns yellow
Ready to leave the tree, its home.
And then one day, it breaks and falls,
Unafraid and peaceful.
It surrenders to nature,
Knows nature is its true mother.

I am like the leaf,
I believe in nature.
I am peaceful with all that happens.

PRACTICE SUMMARY

So far we have learnt some very meaningful concepts and practices. They have made us think again about what happiness really is. They have made us question our ordinary way of thinking and being.

The views in this book that I am presenting to you are taught by enlightened beings and sages. These are very useful to live a happy life and become your own best friend.

But all these concepts will only really be helpful if you practise them and make them a part of your life. You have to actively practise spending time with yourself and becoming more mindful.

On the next page are three examples of the routines you can follow to make mindfulness a part of your everyday life. Follow whichever routine you most like or a different routine each day.

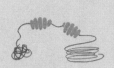

MINDFULNESS ROUTINE 1

- Do the breathing happiness practice for five or ten breaths (page 22) in the morning or whenever you get time.
- Brush or take a shower mindfully during the day (page 38).
- Put aside five minutes of silent time just to be by yourself, doing nothing, in the evening. Just observe all that you see and hear.
- Practise gratitude for two minutes at night. Thank nature for one good thing that happened today (page 42).

MINDFULNESS ROUTINE 2

- Take five mindful breaths in the morning. When you breathe in, feel your belly filling up. When you breathe out, feel your belly going down.
- Eat a fruit or your tiffin in silence and with mindfulness during the day. Pay full attention to every morsel.
- Do the silent island breathing practice (page 35) in the evening.
- Practise gratitude for two minutes before you sleep.

MINDFULNESS ROUTINE 3

- Take ten mindful breaths in the morning. Pay attention to the breath as you feel it in your nostrils. Notice the cool air entering your nostrils and the warm air exiting your nostrils.
- Do one activity you enjoy mindfully during the day. You can listen to a song, cook, paint or go for a walk. Whatever you do, pay full attention to it for the duration of the activity.
- Practise mindfulness of sounds in the evening for two minutes (page 14).
- Practise gratitude in the night for two minutes. Remember all the pleasant and enjoyable situations you encountered today and thank life for making them happen.

REFLECTION SPACE

_____
_____
_____
_____
_____
_____
_____
_____
_____
_____
_____
_____
_____
_____
_____
_____
_____
_____
_____
_____
_____

PART II

MAKING FRIENDS WITH YOUR MIND

A big part of making friends with yourself is making friends with your mind. To make friends with it, you need to understand it. That is what we will attempt in this section.

1

BEGINNING TO EXPLORE WITH YOUR MIND

EXERCISE: HOW DO YOU EXPERIENCE WITH YOUR MIND?

Given below are scenarios you might experience with your mind. You may tick some or even all of them.

- ☐ It speaks to me. I hear an inner voice.
- ☐ It creates thoughts.
- ☐ It is like a storyteller; it comments on people and situations.
- ☐ It is like a movie at times. I see images.
- ☐ It warns me about what I should and should not do.
- ☐ It tells me whether I am doing well or not.
- ☐ It tries to guess what others may be thinking about me.
- ☐ There is more than one voice in my head sometimes: one telling me the right thing to do and the other tempting me to do the opposite.
- ☐ It brings up memories from the past, of good times and bad times.
- ☐ It imagines situations I will face in the future, some pleasant and some unpleasant.

The human mind is all of this and much more. It works non-stop and we know that through our own experience. While we spend so much time listening to our mind, we hardly stop to pause and know it better.

Is there truth in what our mind is saying? What should we believe in and what should we ignore? Do our thoughts make sense all the time? What is it our mind is engaged in most of the time?

These questions can only be answered if we learn to observe our mind closely. So, let us begin exploring our mind and getting to know it better.

The Wandering Mind

The first step in knowing the mind is knowing what it is occupied with. Is it in the present? Or is it somewhere else? If you notice carefully, you will find that while your body is in the present, eating or bathing or lying on the bed, your mind is often wandering or lost in thought. Let us do a short practice now to really see where your mind wanders to.

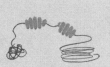

PRACTICE: AWARENESS OF THE WANDERING MIND

Close your eyes for two minutes. Notice whatever thoughts arise then. Just observe the thoughts that come on their own.

Do not try to think of something specific or try to stop a thought. Simply sit quietly, with your eyes closed, and notice the thoughts that come to you.

After two minutes, open your eyes.

Now go over the list below and check which categories your thoughts belonged to.

- **Thoughts of the past:** Thoughts about something that had already happened. For example, thoughts about what you ate last evening or what you did an hour ago.
- **Thoughts of the future:** Thoughts about something that has not yet happened but might happen. For example, what you would do next or what you would like to eat for dinner.
- **Thoughts involving imagination:** Thoughts about scenarios that are not a part of your life. For example, I wish I had longer hair or I wish I had a dog.
- **Thoughts involving commentary:** Thoughts about commenting on something in the present. For example, this exercise is boring or interesting, or a particular sound is unpleasant or too loud and so on.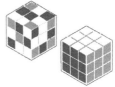

This is a short two-minute exercise, but as you become more aware of your mind, you will notice how your thoughts wander throughout the day.

You will realize that only for very brief periods does your mind stay in the present. You may be brushing, but your mind might be thinking away furiously. You may be bathing or eating, but your mind might not be paying attention to what you are doing at all. Often, you may eat an entire plate of food without really tasting it, or without even realizing how much you have eaten.

It is not only *your* mind that works this way; the minds of all human beings are the same, wandering ever so often. Your mind stays in the present only when you are doing something that requires a lot of focus, like solving a difficult maths problem or listening to music with great interest and attention, hearing every word or note.

Now if your mind drifts only sometimes into the past or future or into the world of imagination, there is no real problem. That is okay and sometimes, even required. The problem occurs when your mind is wandering a lot and you are rarely ever in the present.

What Is the Big Deal about Being in the Present?

Everyone's life is only real in the present, is it not? Wherever you are and whatever you are doing is the only place that is real. The past is over, and the future hasn't arrived yet. Imagination is just that—imaginary and unreal. And commentary is your mind trying to tell you stories about the present. But none of these are the present.

The present is what is *now*, where you are now and whatever you are experiencing now.

Only in the present can you do any action or make a choice. And even the present is changing all the time. Every point in time is a new, fresh moment. The last moment has gone by. It is over. It can never come back. A new moment is here and before you know it, it passes by too.

That is how everyone's life actually is. But we seem to live more in our thoughts about the past and the future, and less in our real life. Is it then possible to enjoy our life if we are not really living it and experiencing it?

Here is the story of Riju that will make this clearer.

Riju, a student of eighth grade, was sitting in his classroom, looking straight at the teacher, who was teaching chemistry. His mind, however, was not dwelling on chemistry at all. He was thinking about his summer holidays, which he had spent at his grandmother's farmhouse. What fun it was. Like when his cousin and he used the spare battery generator to create a waterfall near the pond. How they worked in the sun tirelessly. How lovely the waterfall looked.

Every time his mind came back to the class, he found it so boring. Besides, chemistry was not a subject he much liked and he did not feel like paying it any attention. His mind kept going over mental pictures of the farmhouse and all the things he did there.

What is happening with Riju in this story is common for most of us. We want to escape from a present we find boring into a thought we find interesting and juicy. Now, daydreaming is fine at times. However, if it becomes a habit, particularly of avoiding a boring present by escaping into a daydream, then we have a problem on our hands.

If Riju continues to escape into daydreaming, he will find the present only more difficult to manage. He will start seeking pleasure in enjoyable memories and imagination, and real life will seem very boring. Slowly, his relationship with life will weaken and he will become unhappy.

Riju's was an example of being caught up in thoughts of the past. Let's take another example, this time of being caught up in the future.

Sujata is worried about not doing well in her exams. Her finals are only three days away and she is very nervous. She is concerned that her parents will blame her for watching TV and not studying enough. Her mind is full of images where her mom looks angry and her dad looks disappointed. She fears that they may also quarrel with each other because they both would be so upset. That would be terrible and it will all be her fault.

Where is Sujata's mind wandering? Into the future. Her thoughts are all about the future and they are not happy thoughts at all. She is worrying and imagining the worst outcome possible. However, is this her reality? Has she already done poorly in her exams? Not at all!

In fact, the reality is that her exams have not yet started, and she still has time to study. Sujata is spending excessive amounts of time thinking and worrying about the future instead of using the same time to prepare for her exams.

You see how our thoughts get too focused on the past or future, and just don't let us make the most of our present. Yet, we continue to get caught up in those thoughts, believing in them unknowingly, without awareness. Why? Simply because it is our habit to do so and we have never paused to see if this habit is helpful.

Through our practices in this part of the book, we will train the mind to disentangle from thoughts and to stay focused on the present.

Why not do a practice right away to start the training?

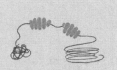

PRACTICE: BREATHING MEDITATION

This is one of the most important practices, and you must try and make it a daily habit.

Sit in a posture that is comfortable and where you don't need to move much. Either sit on the ground cross-legged, or sit in a chair where your feet touch the ground. Keep the feet firmly planted on the ground. See that your back is relaxed but straight.

You are in the right posture for the practice now. You can use this posture for all your meditation practices. Now let's begin.

Close your eyes and take some time to just relax your body. Relax your face, arms, belly and legs, one by one.

Once you feel a little relaxed, start to focus on your breath. Breathing in, simply stay aware of breathing in. Breathing out, stay aware of breathing out.

You can stay aware of your breath in three ways. Choose the way that is easiest for you. You can also try all three ways at different times and decide which one works for you.

1. **Count your breaths:** When you breathe in and breathe out once, count one. The next full round of in-breath and out-breath is counted as two. In this way, you will count up to ten. Once you finish counting ten breaths,

you start again from one. In case, you get distracted and forget your count, you can start from one again.

2. **Feel your breath in the belly:** When you breathe in, your belly rises, and when you breathe out, your belly deflates or falls. Keep your entire attention in the rising and falling of your belly. Keep noticing every breath in your belly. You can add counting to this if you want or you can simply observe the movement of the belly when you breathe.

3. **Feel your breath in your nostrils:** When you breathe in, cool air enters your nostrils. When you breathe out, warm air exits your nostrils. You can feel your breath in your nostrils by noticing how the air feels with each in-breath and each out-breath. You can also focus on where it touches the insides of your nostrils.

While meditating, if you get distracted by thoughts, simply bring your focus back to your breath. Getting distracted is natural and happens often. Don't worry about it. Simply come back to your breath.

Do this practice for five minutes every day. If you feel calm and start enjoying it, you can increase it to ten minutes.

It is very important to remember the purpose of this meditation. You are not trying to get a perfect score. You are only trying to train your mind to stay present. Since the breath is always in the present and always with you, keeping your mind connected to the breath is a great way to stay present.

When you do this practice, you become aware of the number of thoughts that distract you. As you practice focusing on the breath, you are training your brain not to pay attention to the thoughts, but instead to return to the breath, which is in the present. Your brain is learning that distracting thoughts are not important. The present is more important.

Throughout the day, in the same way, keep recognizing when your thoughts take over, when they distract you from what you are doing, and keep returning to the present.

When eating, remind yourself, 'Now I am eating, so let me pay attention to the food.' When bathing, remind yourself, 'Now I am bathing, so let me pay attention to the warm water.' We have also previously learnt this in the section on paying attention (page 36).

2

THE MIND—A STORYTELLER

So far we have learnt that our mind is rarely in the present. It is wandering to the past, the future, caught up in imagination or commenting about the present. Now let us examine what our thoughts are about. What is the content of our thoughts?

Our mind is a storyteller. It thinks in terms of stories. Our mind tells stories about what has happened, what is likely to happen and how it will affect us. Also, judgements about whether we are good enough or others are good or not are part of these stories.

For instance, it can say, 'You were supposed to clean up your room and you haven't; now your mom will be angry.' You listen to this story, believe it and get frustrated with your mom even before she has said anything.

We act and react based on these stories created by the mind because we believe them. But are these stories true?

The Story Is Not the Truth

Often, we confuse the story told by our mind, with the truth. Let us understand this through an example.

Suhani believes she is the teacher's favourite. Her teacher is always praising her and putting in good remarks in her report card. This makes her think that the teacher likes her very much.

Then one day, the annual school play is announced. The teacher calls out the names of the students who will play different parts in the play. Suhani is quite sure that her teacher will select her for the lead role. But she does not get selected. Instead, she gets a somewhat unimportant role in the play.

She begins to feel uneasy. She feels cheated and betrayed. She feels like her teacher does not like her any more. She develops a lot of self-doubt, which means she starts to question whether she is good enough or not.

Now, since we are outsiders to Suhani's life, we can study the situation objectively. We can see that the stories created by her mind are not true. Her teacher may still like her, but that does not mean she will give her the lead part in the annual play. Others deserve a chance to play lead roles too. And perhaps, somebody else is just a better fit for that role.

However, Suhani does not see it this way because her mind is wrapped up in this story about being the teacher's favourite. To her, being the teacher's favourite means getting the teacher's attention and favour at all times. When something happens that does not fit into her story, she judges herself as not good enough and becomes miserable, unhappy and full of self-doubt.

For us, it is important to contemplate this: Is Suhani unhappy because of the actual situation or because of the stories her mind is telling her? Isn't it her mind's story, which says, 'I am the teacher's favourite and, therefore, I must get the lead role', that is making her unhappy? Not only is that story untrue but it is also very self-centred and unfair.

The actual situation is just the truth. One person cannot get all the attention. There is a class full of people who will get selected for different things at different times and it is natural for it to be this way.

But in her mind, it means that she is not liked enough, and that she is not good enough. She feels disappointed with herself, upset with the teacher, jealous of the person who got the lead role, and overall, has a miserable day at school.

She could also continue to feel upset when she gets back home. She may vent her frustration on her brother, sister or parents, or she may just quietly sulk alone. She may even feel distressed the next day and not want to go to school.

All this because her mind made up an unreal story about her not being good enough and she believed it.

Do you see how unhappy believing the mind's story can make us? Even a story like 'I am the teacher's favourite', which actually seems like a positive thought, can make us feel glum.

Getting Free from the Trap of Untrue Mental Stories

So, what shall we do so that we don't find ourselves trapped in our mind's stories?

The most important thing we need to understand is that not everything our mind says is the truth. Here, mindfulness of our thoughts, which is our ability to observe thoughts objectively or neutrally is very useful. When we are mindful, we become *aware* when a thought occupies our mind. We also become aware that it is telling a story. We can then have some space to decide wisely whether to believe in it or not.

If Suhani were to practise mindfulness, she may still feel some disappointment about not being chosen for the lead role, but quite soon, she would become aware that this is just a story, not the truth. In fact, she would even understand that competing with everyone for popularity and attention is unhelpful and is making her unhappy. She may be able to let go of the unhappy thoughts and feelings sooner. This may help her to play the role given to her with more acceptance and enjoyment.

When she practises like this, over time, she may even learn to feel happy for the people who got the role instead of her. She may understand that everyone deserves to do well, not just her. She could slowly learn to be happy in the happiness of others. What a peaceful way to live!

Reading Suhani's story, you may realize that your mind too creates stories and doubts in you. It may make you believe that you are great, at times. At other times, it may tell you, you are no good.

You have to learn to let go of these stories and judgements created by the mind in favour of the truth.

The truth is more reasonable. The truth says, 'Hey, you are not the greatest person around and you don't need to be that. You are not the worst person around either and you don't need to worry. You are just you—unique, different, not better than or worse than anyone. Others are also just unique, different people. So, be happy and enjoy being you.'

Over the years, since I've been doing my meditation practice regularly, I have become closer to this truth. Even now, sometimes my mind's stories take over, but I am able to quickly return to the present and realize that they are not the truth.

I feel so much happier now having practised this in my life and staying more connected to the truth.

This story-creating tendency of the mind is universal. It happens to everyone. If people do not question the stories of their mind, they end up becoming unhappy or happy based on the story rather than the truth.

Here is a story of a wise farmer who accepts the present and does not believe in the stories created by anyone's mind.

MAYBE

Once upon a time, there was a wise old farmer who had worked his crops for many years. One day, his horse ran away. Upon hearing the news, his neighbours came to visit. 'Such bad luck,' they said sympathetically.

'Maybe,' replied the farmer.

The next morning, the horse returned, bringing with it three other wild horses. 'How wonderful!' exclaimed the neighbours. 'Now you have three more horses!'

'Maybe,' replied the old man.

The following day, his son tried to ride one of the new horses. That horse was untamed and his son was thrown off the horse and he broke his leg. The neighbours came to offer their sympathy once again. 'How sad,' they said. 'Your son is hurt!'

'Maybe,' answered the farmer.

The day after, military officials came to the village to enrol young men into the army. Seeing that the son's leg was broken, they did not ask him to join. The neighbours congratulated the farmer on his good luck, saying his son was lucky to stay home with him and did not have to leave and join the army.

'Maybe,' said the farmer.

What does this story tell us? The neighbours have usual storytelling minds where they are constantly judging situations as good or bad.

But the farmer is wise and non-judgemental. He does not believe in the stories. He understands that life keeps changing. What may seem like a boon today, may become a curse tomorrow. What may seem like a problem today, may end up being a blessing later.

So, he accepts the present situation for whatever it is. He does not get trapped in the mind's stories of what *has* happened or what *will* happen. He does not judge situations as good or bad.

To learn to be like this farmer, we need to develop a beginner's mind.

Developing a Beginner's Mind

A beginner is someone who does something for the first time. Similarly, a beginner's mind is a mind that is able to see things as though they are being seen for the first time. Everything is seen afresh, without being judged as good or bad. It is a mindset of non-judgement that can be developed through training.

To understand this easily, simply look at the book you are reading. Look at it as if you don't know what it is. Try to look at it as though you are seeing it for the first time.

See the colours, the font, the design, the titles. Notice its thickness, its texture and how it feels in your hand.

You almost never pay attention to anything in this way. Since you know it is a book, you usually do not see it afresh.

Now imagine applying this mindset to people and situations.

Sometimes, you meet people, and your mind may say, 'Oh, they are so boring, I don't like them.' Instead, if you simply try to experience what is happening in the present, you may actually have a better time with them.

Let's suppose your parents want you to accompany them to a relative's house, where you usually get quite bored. You don't want to go with them. Instead, you want to hang out with your friends. Your parents, however, won't take no for an answer and you just have to go.

Now there are two options for you. You pull a face and go with them arguing, sulking and grumpy. As expected, you don't have a good time.

Or, you use the beginner's mind way of approaching the situation. This is the way of non-judgement. You choose to not let your mind dominate you and call the entire experience boring. Instead, you take it moment by moment and pay attention to the present.

For instance, if there is dinner, you choose to pay attention to the experience of eating and enjoy the food; if there is a terrace or a balcony, you choose to stand there and enjoy the surrounding sights and sounds.

In reality, there are so many things to experience. However, when the mind considers a situation as boring, it colours the reality and all you can feel is bored.

Now that you understand the beginner's mind, you will always have a choice. You can unwisely choose to go with the mind's judgemental story or you can wisely choose to stay with the actual experience, which is the reality of the present moment.

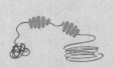

PRACTICE: DEVELOPING A BEGINNER'S MIND

Here is a practice that will help you develop a beginner's mind. Read the contemplative poem below for inspiration and then follow the suggestions given for the practice.

LOOKING MINDFULLY

As I mindfully look,
I start to clearly see
The flowers on the roadside bush,
The little newborn puppy,
It has a grey paw,
The bee dances nearby,
Water ripples in the puddles,
Clouds float in a quiet sky.

I see, I don't judge, I watch in silent practice
As the world comes alive, beautiful and miraculous.

After reading this verse, look around. What do you see? Try not to judge anything as boring or interesting. Simply observe. Look at the objects around you. What is stationary? Is something moving? Watch the movement.

What do you see in the distance? The road? Trees? Are the leaves moving?

Look deeply at the colours of the objects you notice. Try to look at everything as if it is new to you, as though you are seeing it for the first time.

This is the meditation of observing our surroundings with a beginner's mind. We learn to watch everything with a certain freshness until we become deeply aware of our surroundings. It is such a beautiful way to stay connected to the world and not be lost in thought.

3

NEGATIVITY BIAS: LOOKING FOR NEGATIVES

Do you know that human beings have many more negative thoughts than positive ones? We are more likely to find fault with others than appreciate them. We are more likely to be upset about a challenging situation than be happy about a joyful one.

Do you know why this happens? Because of a tendency of our mind known as 'negativity bias'. Negativity bias is a tendency to both remember and look for negatives.

Here are some more examples:

- We remember a situation where someone has been mean to us better than a situation when someone was kind to us.
- When we lose a game or race, or when we make a mistake in a performance, we remember it better than the instances where we have done well.
- Painful memories are clearer to us than those that are pleasant.
- When we have an exam or a football game coming up, we have more fear of what could go wrong than thoughts of what could go right.

The biggest sign perhaps is that our mind is more often rolling in unpleasant thoughts rather than pleasant ones.

If you observe your thoughts as we did earlier in this part, you will find this to be true.

Why Is Knowing about Negativity Bias Useful?

We need to know about our tendency to dwell too much on negatives so that we can quickly recognize and change this way of thinking.

If we allow our mind to wallow in negative thinking, we will naturally become unhappier with time. We will increasingly become bitter, angry or grumpy. In time, we may also get depressed.

Imagine, how much of our precious time in life is spent with negative thoughts, simply because we do not know our mind and how to be friends with it.

Here are three steps we can take to change negativity bias:

1. We can *recognize* negative thoughts and remind ourselves that they are not necessarily true; that negative thinking is just a human tendency.
2. We can learn to *let go* of such thinking through mindfulness and meditation, by bringing our attention to the present repeatedly.
3. We can *train* our mind to think in a healthy way by appreciating all the good in our life and by practising gratitude.

When you practice mindfulness during the day, you are already practising letting go of negative thinking. If you practice breathing meditation (page 67) regularly and letting go of thoughts during your practice, your mind will start cleansing itself of all unwanted negative thoughts.

4

YOUR THOUGHTS ARE NOT POWERFUL; YOU ARE!

Who Is Driving Your Car?

This question is very valid when we are working with thoughts. Are you in charge or are your thoughts in charge? Are you driving your car or are your thoughts in the driving seat, while you sit feeling helpless in the passenger seat?

Often, our thoughts overpower us. They tell us what to do. They keep visiting us again and again, telling us fabricated or made-up stories. Stories of how we are not loved, how we are not making our parents happy, how our friends do not think well of us, how we must have something more to be happy and so on.

We forget that these are just thoughts—impermanent, ever-changing creations of our mind. Just visitors that come and go. They are not us.

Sometimes our thoughts are like quiet whispers, but at other times, they are so loud that they can drive us crazy. They only have that power because we don't treat them like visitors that have come for some time and will leave in some time. We treat them as super important. We offer them the driver's seat.

Let us take a scenario and examine it deeply to understand how we end up giving a lot of power to a thought.

Let's suppose that once when you were chatting with some friends, one of them talked about how much they were enjoying playing the latest video game.

Until this point, you did not know this game even existed or did not care much for it. Then a thought entered your mind: 'I should try this game. It will be fun.'

Was this thought powerful already? Not really. It was just a thought like a visitor who had just walked in.

Later, when you got home, you asked your parents to buy you the game. They refused.

Now let us see what happened at the thought level when your parents refused to buy you the game. Your mind created a story. It said, 'This seems to be a great game. Your friends have it. You must get it. Your parents are not understanding this. This is unfair.'

Now how powerful did the thought become? Quite powerful! You gave the initial mild thought—'I would like to play this game'—a lot of attention and belief. You allowed it to occupy your mind. What is worse, you fully believed that having the game is the only way you could become happier. This is nothing but fiction. This kind of belief made your thought stronger.

What happened next? You got annoyed at your parents because they refused. You sulked, you got frustrated and irritable. Now your thought had fully occupied the driving seat. It had become too powerful. You had very little control over it and it drove you crazy. Your thought had taken charge of your feelings, without you even knowing it.

You see how a simple thought can develop into a very powerful one and make us lose our peace of mind?

You were happy enough before you'd ever heard of the game. How could possessing the game then become so important suddenly? It only became important because you did not question your thoughts. You just believed in them.

So, who has the power then: you or your thoughts? The reality is that you have the ultimate power. You can choose to give your thought attention and belief and make it a monster that occupies your mind, or you can simply let it go and give it less power to upset you.

You cannot control whether a thought will arise or not.

But you can smile at it and let it pass. You can remind yourself that it is just a thought, not necessarily the truth.

All the mindfulness practices that you have been doing so far, will help you with this.

5

HOW TO HANDLE DIFFICULT THOUGHTS

So far we have dealt with the problematic aspects of our mind, but our mind is amazing too and so very useful.

Think of the mind as a sharp tool, like a knife. If you know how to use the knife well, you can cut fruits, make salads and do some really creative things.

However, in the hands of someone who does not know that the knife is a sharp object, it can be dangerous. It can hurt and even seriously harm them.

It is the same with your mind. If you understand it and use it well, it is a good companion. In fact, your mind is helping you to learn all the concepts and practices in this book. You use your mind to study, learn music, paint, learn a sport and so much more. It helps you in so many ways.

However, if you don't understand it, it can harm you by fabricating stories, creating false judgements and keeping you dissatisfied and entrenched in the cycle of dukkha (see page 9).

Wise sages across centuries have said that the one who knows how to work with their mind knows how to live a happy life!

You have learnt a lot about your mind so far. Now let's use this knowledge to work with thoughts that are difficult for you to deal with.

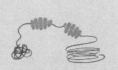

PRACTICE: MINDFULNESS OF DIFFICULT THOUGHTS

Take a difficult thought that you often struggle with. If you cannot think of something right now, come back to this activity when you are struggling with a difficult thought.

Describe the difficult thought in some detail here:

_____

_____

_____

_____

_____

_____

Now follow the three steps given below:

1. **Remind yourself:**

- This thought is merely a passing visitor. It is impermanent. If I don't give it much attention, it will fade away.
- This thought is not necessarily the truth. It is a story that my mind has created. I do not have to believe in it.
- This thought is negative because human beings have a tendency to have more negative thoughts than positive ones. It is not my fault that I am stuck with such a difficult thought.

2. **Don't add to the thought:**

    When you understand that it is only a thought, make a conscious attempt to avoid adding to the thought. Not adding to the thought means that you don't add another thought to the already existing one.

    For example, if this thought crosses your mind: *I want to go overnight to a friend's place and my parents are not allowing me*, don't add to it by thinking more thoughts like, *Other parents are better than mine. My friend's parents are so friendly and understanding, they even bought him a bike. My parents are always so negative, they never understand me.*
    These are thoughts that you add on without realizing and a false story starts to form in your mind.

3. **Return to the present:**

    Once you have reminded yourself about the true nature of your thoughts and chosen to not add on any thoughts, it is time to choose the present instead of the thought.
    You can ask yourself: *Where am I now? What am I doing now? How can I pay attention to what is happening right now in my life instead of paying attention to the thought?*
    In order to return to the present, you can take three deep breaths mindfully, pay attention to sounds or to whatever activity you are involved in.

If you have some space, you can do the silent island practice (page 35) or the breathing meditation practice too (page 67).

Remember, this is not a one-time practice. The same thought may recur again and again. In fact, difficult thoughts are particularly sticky. You may have to follow the above steps each time the thought recurs.

When you do this practice once, the thought will most likely subside for a while. However, within minutes, as you stop paying attention to what is happening in the present, it will resurface. You will need to repeat these steps as often as the thought bothers you.

6

METTA: A POWERFUL ANTIDOTE FOR THE JUDGEMENTAL MIND

Do you know what an antidote is? If someone has been poisoned by taking in something that is bad or toxic for them, a quick antidote is given to counteract or reverse the effects of the poison.

When we start to observe our minds, we may find ourselves dealing with toxic thoughts or judgements. Our thoughts may involve disliking ourselves or others, commenting negatively on situations, wishing ill for some people, thinking of revenge and so on. Such thoughts are full of unhappiness. They are definitely not healthy thoughts to have.

So far we have learnt certain very helpful ways of looking at these thoughts—viewing them objectively, exercising wisdom before believing in them, choosing to focus on the present instead of the thought and so on.

Now, in addition to these, we are also going to learn a practice that is an antidote to the negative thoughts in the mind. This is the beautiful and gentle practice of metta. Practising metta will reduce our unhealthy tendency to judge ourselves and others and increase our ability to be kind.

Just as neem juice is bitter but can clean our system from the inside, metta may be initially difficult to practice, but over time it will cleanse our mind.

The Practice of Metta

Metta is a practice of feeling compassion and kindness for ourselves and others.

The word 'metta' is a Pali word. In Sanskrit, the word is *maitri*. Both these words mean friendliness. In that sense, it is a practice of being friendly towards ourselves and others. Hence, it is an ideal practice for making friends with ourselves.

Let us start this practice now. It is a slightly detailed practice. Read through it fully and try to understand it before you begin.

PRACTICE: METTA

Sit comfortably in a chair, on the ground or on your bed. Support your back with cushions so you can fully relax. Take a few breaths mindfully.

Now read this contemplative poem before starting your practice.

THE SUN

I see the sun
I see its light and feel its warmth.
Deep kindness in its heart as it wakes up the world
Giving light to all—
The poor and the rich,
The strong and the weak.
It discriminates against no one.
It strengthens the bones of all creatures
And gives plants their food.
Its friendliness is beyond words,
It has true metta.

I am like the sun
I feel deep metta, kindness towards all.
I want all to be well and happy.

Now read the poem again slowly, understanding every sentence and feeling it.

Feeling this poem is a crucial part of the practice. Once you have read it with some feeling, close your eyes.

Imagine that there is a warm and kind sun inside your chest and its rays are reaching out to the whole world lovingly.

This sun does not discriminate at all. Its light and warmth are meant for everyone. It is very friendly to every being.

Enjoy this light and warmth within you for a few breaths.

Now follow these three steps:

Step 1:

Bring an image of yourself to your mind. Look at this image of yourself with a lot of kindness. Just like all other creatures, you have a life that has joys and sorrows. Sometimes you feel joyful, and sometimes, you go through difficulties and feel low. You need your own kindness and friendliness.

Imagine sending yourself some light and warmth that you generated when reading the poem.

In your mind, make a wish for yourself: 'May I be happy. May I be well. May I feel light in my heart. May things become easy for me.'

As you wish this for yourself, you are giving love and friendliness to yourself. You are giving metta to yourself. It is such a wonderful feeling to wish well for yourself. Enjoy this feeling for a few breaths.

Step 2:

Now, imagine all the beings in the world. People from countries near and far. The young, the elderly, children and infants. People living in big cities and small villages. People speaking so many different languages.

Imagine the various animals, birds, insects and trees that exist in this world. All of them need kindness and friendliness. All of them have lives that can be difficult. All of them struggle for food and their livelihoods, while facing dangers and challenges.

Imagine this whole world in your mind's eye and wish happiness for all: 'May all be happy. May all be well. May all feel light in their hearts. May things become easy for everyone.'

The first few times you do this practice, you can end the practice at this point and open your eyes.

When you are new to the practice, just the first two steps are enough. When you do the metta practice several times and feel more confident, you can add the third step. This is a difficult but very powerful step.

Step 3:

Once again, remind yourself that you are like the sun, sending all these friendly rays across the world. You are sending them high into the sky and the mountains, deep into the ocean to all the creatures there.

It is so wonderful to care for all. Enjoy this feeling for a few breaths. Just like the sun does not discriminate about who receives its light and warmth, you too will try not to discriminate. You will send it to everyone. People who are good to you and those who are not.

Now, think of a person you don't like very much.

Bring to your mind a picture of this person. Perhaps this person has hurt you or has been mean and unkind to you.

Remind yourself that this person, too, has a mind just like yours and everyone else's. A mind that tells unkind, untrue stories and makes them suffer and feel low.

They also feel sad, jealous, unhappy, afraid and angry, like all human beings.

Just like you sent warmth, light and friendliness to all creatures in the world, try to give your warmth and friendliness to this difficult person.

Wish for this person: 'Like all other beings, may you be well. May you be happy. May you be light in your heart. May things become easy for you.'

Stay silent and aware of how you are feeling for a few minutes.

Even if you cannot feel friendliness for this person, it is okay. At least, you tried. The trying itself is a real change. You were able to put aside your anger and judgement for some time and honestly try. That is all that is needed for this practice. A genuine attempt.

This part of the practice is the real antidote.

Here is a beautiful story about metta and compassion.

THE NATURE OF THINGS

Two monks were washing bowls in a river when they noticed a scorpion that was drowning. One monk immediately scooped it up and set it on the bank. In the process, he was stung by the scorpion.

He went back to washing his bowl and the scorpion fell in again. The monk saved the scorpion once more and was stung a second time.

The other monk asked him, 'Friend, why do you continue to save the scorpion when you know its nature is to sting?'

'Because,' the monk replied, 'to save it is my nature.'

The monk realizes there is nothing *personal* about the scorpion's sting. The scorpion's nature is to be afraid and to sting out of that fear.

The monk realizes that the scorpion's mind is creating fear and making it attack even those who want to save it. This wise and correct understanding allows the monk to continue feeling kind towards the scorpion even though it hurts him. It is very helpful to try to see the world as the monk sees it.

Some people in our life attack us like this. They hurt us or bully us. We can try to see their behaviour as emerging from their mind's unhealthy habits. When we can see it like that, we get less upset with them.

Even if we need to keep a distance from them, we can still stay compassionate and friendly towards them, in our hearts. Our own unhappiness is also significantly reduced when we don't hold negative feelings towards the difficult people in our lives.

PRACTICE SUMMARY

The best gift you can give anyone else is a happy and peaceful you. Think of the people you really like and who make you happy. They may even be your pet or your friends.

What makes you happy? Their happiness. Their freshness. Their freedom and their joy when they see you. You see, happiness is inside us, but it is easily felt by those outside us.

Similarly, unhappiness is also inside us but can be easily felt by those outside us. When someone is unhappy or in pain, they may talk grumpily, snap at others, criticize others or look sad. Slowly, we also start becoming unhappy in their company and start staying away from them.

So, being happy is not only great for us but also for others.

If you regularly practise what you have been learning in this section and make non-judgement and metta a part of your life, you will find that you feel naturally happier as days go by.

Here are the practices that you can do regularly from this section. You can now let go of the mindfulness routines suggested at the end of Part I and instead follow the practices given below.

1. **Breathing meditation (page 67):** You can do this practice regularly, preferably every day for five minutes to start with. You can increase this to seven or ten minutes or even longer if you can manage. Longer practices help the mind to settle better and provide more benefit. However, starting with a shorter practice is perfectly fine. If you feel too restless, sit for some time with restlessness, then you can stop your practice. Remember not to make your practice

a chore to do but an enjoyable time to spend hanging out with yourself and understanding your mind.

2. **Metta practice (page 89):** This is the second most important practice. You can do the metta practice once every two or three days. On the days you practise metta, it is okay not to do the breathing meditation, especially if it gets too much for you. However, if you feel comfortable, you can always practice metta after breathing meditation. In fact, you can combine the practices when you become familiar with both and don't need the instructions any more.

3. **Mindfulness of thoughts:** This is not per se a practice to sit and do for some time. This is something for you to remember as you go through your day and your life. Every time you feel caught up in the stories created by the mind, you need to realize that they may not be the whole truth. Let them go and return your attention to the present.

4. **Mindfulness of difficult thoughts (page 85):** This practice need not be done regularly. You can do this practice only when you are struggling with a difficult, recurring thought.

Below are the practices you should continue from Part I:

1. **Appreciating yourself every day (page 31):** Every day appreciate something about yourself. Acknowledge something good about you.

2. **Gratitude practice (page 42):** Every night before you sleep, take a minute to thank nature for something good that happened during the day.

If you are regular with the breathing meditation practice in this part, you can let go of the silent island visualization practice (page 35) in part I. However, if you are finding breathing meditation difficult, then please continue with the silent island practice daily.

REFLECTION SPACE

_____

_____

_____

_____

_____

_____

_____

_____

_____

_____

_____

_____

_____

_____

_____

_____

_____

_____

_____

_____

PART III

MAKING FRIENDS
WITH YOUR BODY

In the two previous sections, we learnt how to become friendly towards ourselves and our mind. In this section, we will direct our attention to our body and learn to be friends with it. In order to be friends with your body, it is crucial to understand what it is saying. How can we understand what the body is saying? By learning the art of listening to it.

Yes, our body speaks to us! It has its own vocabulary, a vocabulary of sensations. A language of sensations that we can definitely learn with some regular practice.

You probably already understand a little intuitively. You know when your body tells you it's hungry, thirsty or tired. How do you know that? You can sense it, right? Through a stream of sensations, your body expresses hunger, thirst, tiredness, happiness, sadness and most other states. When we start paying attention to the body, we can learn this language of sensations and truly make friends with our body.

But just as we listen with focus to learn any language, we have to do the same with the body's language.

So, let us turn our attention to our body with a simple exercise.

1

CONNECTING WITH THE BODY

Stand up straight and take three deep breaths. Now start bending forward.

How far can you go? Don't push yourself too much; go just as far as you can. Now, observe that you automatically know where to stop. With some effort, you may be able to go a little further without causing too much pain, but you won't be able to stretch beyond that. Right? You know all this because your body is talking to you. It is telling you what it can do and how far you can go.

Now stand up straight again and start bending backward. Perhaps you can bend backward even lesser than you could bend forward. You immediately know where to stop.

Do you have to think about all this specifically? No! Your body tells you, and you just listen to it. These are the obvious ways in which our body talks. It gives you sensations like pain or tightness to express that you cannot move any more in a certain direction. You listen to those sensations and respond.

Your body spoke loud and clear when it came to bending forward and backward. However, often, the body also just whispers and speaks very quietly. It means that it speaks in very mild sensations, those we are not used to sensing easily.

For instance, when you feel low, you might find that there are body sensations like your chest feeling tight or heavy or your breath feeling short when you are tense.

However, only when we listen closely and patiently to the body can we hear these quieter messages of our body. We are going to develop that ability to listen to the quieter sensations of the body in this section.

Why Should You Bother Listening to the Quieter Messages of Your Body?

When you start understanding the language of sensations, you will know what the body is saying. This will let you recognize when your body is uneasy and try to help it. Here are some reasons why connecting to the body is very important.

1. Your body is always taking care of you

Let us take an example. When there is a loud sound, you quickly shut your ears without hesitation. You did not know where the sound came from. You did not even have time to think. Yet, your body immediately responded and helped you close your ears. It protected your ears from possible damage due to this loud sound.

Similarly, if some food enters the windpipe, there is choking and coughing. This is the body's automatic response to stop the food from entering the windpipe, which can be very dangerous for you. Here, it takes action without you even thinking about it.

This is all possible because of the autonomic nervous system, a part of the nervous system in the body. This system sees that your heart keeps beating, that your digestion continues and that your breathing does not stop even when sleeping. It is always aware of any danger you are in. It is always watching out for you and taking care of you, even without you knowing it.

Even while you are lost in thought, your body is very aware and always doing its job. It is already your friend. Now by paying attention to it, you return its friendship and try to take care of it and support it when it needs you to.

2. Your body is very intelligent and wise

'Listen to your heart.' 'Listen to your gut.'

We often hear people saying such phrases. What do they mean by these? They are simply saying that your heart is wise, your body and gut are also wise. Listen to them! They know what is right. While your mind can make up a lot of stories, your body speaks the truth. Your body contains your quiet inner voice of wisdom.

Have you ever had a situation where you have a strong urge to eat that extra sweet that is tempting but unhealthy? Or gossip about your friend to others? Deep within yourself, you seem to know that it is not the right thing to do. This knowing, which comes from deep within you, is the body's message. This knowing is what your gut communicates.

Think of another situation. Maybe you are binge-watching a TV show or playing a lot of games on your computer. Deep inside, you know that it is time to rest, but your mind is glued to the TV or the computer. Your mind wants more, but your body feels it is enough.

When we seek pleasure and give in to our temptations, it is often because we are not listening to our bodies. Listening to our body is about being guided by our body, by our inner wisdom. However, this voice is not easily clear to us. It is a soft voice. We must really practise paying attention to the body to be able to hear this voice.

3.   Your body is always in the present

Your body is always here, no matter how much your mind wanders. So, noticing and coming back to the body is an excellent way of coming back to the present. Staying aware of the body helps you get away from the mind's stories that are not needed right now. In fact, you have already started noticing the body in your practices so far, where you observed the breath. When you feel your breath in the nostrils or in the belly, you start to connect with the body through these areas. This helps you to be in the present.

4.   Your body knows your emotions and feelings very well

There is a reason why this section comes before the 'Making Friends with Your Feelings' section. To understand your feelings and emotions clearly, you first need to relate to the body's sensations.

Let us see how this happens. Have you ever felt anxious before an exam? How do you know you are feeling anxious? You may say that you just know it, but the truth is that your body feels nervous. You experience some uneasiness in your stomach; your hands may shake or feel sweaty. There are also many milder sensations you are not aware of, but they are all there—and that is how you know you feel nervous. Your nervousness is not just in your mind; it is also very much in your body.

Even sensations of love and happiness are felt in the body. When a friend is kind to you, you feel happy and loved. If you notice your body at such a time, you will know that you feel so open and warm inside your body. Your heart feels light, your face feels sensations of happiness.

When we learn to listen to our bodies, we are better able to know our emotions and deal with them. You will learn about this in the next section.

But for now, let us start listening to this amazing and intelligent body right away!

PRACTICE: LISTENING AND SAYING 'WHAT'S UP' TO THE BODY

When you meet your friends, you greet them by saying, 'Hi' or 'What's up'. This is a natural thing you do with friends. Now let's try to do this with the body. Ask your body, 'Hey, what's up? How are you doing?' If you ask that question while paying attention to your body, it will surely answer. Only, it will answer in terms of sensations.

Now for two minutes, simply pay attention to your body. Just allow yourself to sense what is going on with it.

If you pay attention, you will know whether it feels energetic or tired, tight or loose, tense or relaxed, happy or sad. You have to make a genuine attempt and then wait and observe patiently. It will also tell you whether it needs to sit or stand or lie down, whether it is hungry or not.

You dress the body and clean it, but never spend time listening to it. When you listen to it in this way, your body recognizes you are interested in it and starts to connect with you. It knows you care, and you are listening. It starts to see you as a friend and knows it is loved. It blooms and flourishes because it is happy that you care.

You can do this many times in the day. Just ask your body, 'Hey, how are you?' and spend two minutes quietly trying to see how your body is feeling. Accept whatever it is feeling. It will be happy just because you checked in to say hi.

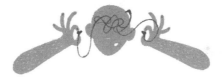

2

SUPPORTING THE BODY

Once you start listening to the body, it will tell you how it is feeling. It will also tell you when you are tired, sleepy or in pain. Once you listen to what your body is going through, you must give it the support it needs. That is being a good friend.

Here are some short practices you can do to quickly show support to your body. These will only take a minute each, but they will communicate to your body that you care for it.

1. One-minute grounding

Often, our bodies become tense, afraid, angry or just confused. The one-minute grounding practice is beneficial in such instances. Grounding means stabilizing or balancing oneself through connecting with an object.

One object that is easily accessible to you—which you constantly are in touch with—is the floor or the ground itself. This ground is stable and steady, and it is only because of this you can stand tall and walk. So, in this one minute, notice the ground underneath your feet. Take a minute to just feel how your feet are touching the ground, how they are connecting with it. Can you feel the hard, steadiness of the earth beneath? One minute later, you can simply return to what you were doing.

You can also use the arms of a chair to 'ground' yourself through your hands. Sit in a chair with an armrest and let your arms completely rest on the chair. As you are sitting, simply let your body relax in the chair. Notice how the connection with the chair feels. You will find that the hard steadiness of the arms of the chair is supportive. Feel the support completely. Observe this for a minute.

You can use this grounding practice through the touch of any stable object. A bench, a chair, the ground or even something you are holding, like a pen. Just pay full attention to what you are touching for a while.

To give you an example, a ten-year-old boy, learning mindfulness, used grounding during one of his tennis matches when he was feeling nervous. He decided to pay attention to the feel of the racquet in his hands for some time, instead of worrying about winning or losing. He said he felt free to enjoy and play the match afterward.

Grounding gives us strength and stability. It brings our focus back to the present and makes our body realize that it is supported by the objects we touch and feel.

2. One-minute self-touch support

You can actually support your body by touching it. We will work more on this in the next section, when we are making friends with our feelings.

For now, simply place a hand on your chest. Tell your body, 'I am there for you. I am supporting you. I can take care of you just as you take care of me.' Stay like that for a minute, noticing all the sensations in the area where your hands connect to your chest. You can do this while sitting in a relaxed position or while lying down. See how your body feels when it is supported by you like this. Does it relax under your touch? Does it feel warm and comfortable? We keep looking out for support from others, but it rarely occurs to us that we can support ourselves lovingly. This practice is the beginning of learning to support yourself by supporting your body.

3. **One-minute movement and stretching support**

As you start listening to the sensations in your body, you will begin to realize that the body sometimes feels very tight and tense or stiff and uneasy. You can then learn to move your body very slowly by listening to exactly what it needs. You move your body anyway, right? You move your body to do something you want. You use your hands to pick things up; you use your legs when you want to walk and go somewhere.

But to support your body, you need to move it slowly. Every movement that you do must be a mindful and conscious one. Why is that?

Because only when you are fully tuned in to your body can you know what it needs. And only when you are fully mindful can you know what part needs to move and how much. When you are slow and patient, you give yourself time to tune in and sense the body and its needs correctly.

Remember, in this practice, we are not just trying to move the body, we are moving in a way the body wants us to move. For example, maybe the body is tight and it wants us to open up our fingers and slowly stretch our hands. Or perhaps, it wants us to rotate our ankles and stretch our legs. I know you may find it difficult to understand what your body wants now, but our practice is to develop precisely this understanding.

Let us do this practice together now.

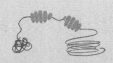

PRACTICE: ONE—MINUTE MOVEMENT AND STRETCHING SUPPORT

Take a few deep breaths while quietly and patiently observing the body. What does it need right now? Does it want you to move or be still? Does it want you to stretch or hug yourself or move your hands or legs?

Maybe it wants you to do nothing; in that case, simply notice the breathing. If you feel like moving in any way, do it very slowly and mindfully with full awareness. After doing this for a minute, come back to this book.

How was this practice for you? Did you notice the body communicating what it needs? Write about your experience here:

_____
_____
_____
_____

3

BODY SCAN PRACTICE: RELAXING AND NOTICING THE BODY

The body scan practice is where you deliberately take time to relax and connect with your body. This is also a proper meditation practice that needs you to dedicate some time to it. It is probably the best practice to really become friends with your body.

In this practice, you will relax and pay full attention to your body. People often think relaxing the body means watching TV, reading a book, or just sitting lazily and daydreaming. In this practice, however, you are going to get the body to rest at a very deep level.

You will do this by paying full attention to each and every part of the body and resting it on purpose. You will gradually move from one part to the next, staying completely aware of sensations in each part of your body. If you make this practice a habit, it will be of tremendous help to you when you work with your feelings next.

Ask a friend or family member to read this aloud to you as you do this practice. Or record it in your own voice. Or simply read it several times so you understand the practice before you do it.

Let us begin.

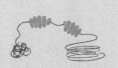

PRACTICE: BODY SCAN

- Lie down on your bed or on a yoga mat if you have one.
- Lie flat on your back comfortably, with your arms a little away from your body and your legs spread apart a bit. Gently close your eyes.
- Now, in this very relaxing posture, take a few deep breaths. Notice each breath entering from the nostrils, travelling through the body and filling your belly. Then notice the breath leaving the abdomen, travelling through the body and coming out from the nostrils. In this way, with your full attention, take five breaths.
- Now, bring your attention to your face and head. Feel these areas of your body.

Even though you are not touching or seeing your face, you can still feel it. You can feel your nose, lips, mouth and all parts of the face because there are some sensations on the face. For instance, how do you know you have a nose? You can feel it, right? Maybe you can feel some vibration or tingling; perhaps you can feel your breath entering and leaving your nostrils. In some way, you can feel your nose. Similarly, you can also feel all other parts of the face.

The sensations may be challenging to feel in the beginning. Remember, it is a new language you are trying to learn. The sensations may be very quiet or not easy to feel. But if you pay attention, you will be able to connect with them in some time.

There may be warmth or coolness in that part of the body. Maybe a sense of something moving, flowing, a vibration or some tingling. Perhaps some heaviness or lightness. All these are sensations that the body constantly experiences. When you connect with them, you learn to connect with the body.

So, for a while, simply pay attention to the face and the entire area of the head. Feel your head, forehead, eyes, nose, mouth, ears and chin.

- Now, once you are done with the face and head, slowly move your attention to your neck.

Notice both the front and back of your neck and also your throat. Maybe you can feel yourself swallowing or the moisture in the throat. You may also feel some more sensations in the neck area.

- After the neck, move your attention to the right arm, starting from the shoulder and noticing the entire arm: upper arm, lower arm and all the fingers.
- Similarly, move to the left arm now.
- Once the arms are done, move to the entire front area of the upper body that includes your chest and belly. Start by resting your attention on the chest. Once you feel some sensation there, move to the area just below it and then to the belly area.

- Once this is done, move to the back of the body and observe your entire back, starting from the shoulder blades to upper back, middle back and lower back.
- Now, notice the seat of the body and the groin area and, from there, move on to the legs.
- Notice the right leg beginning from the hip and notice each part of the leg as you go right down to the toes.
- Similarly, notice the left leg from the top of the leg right down to the toes.

This concludes one whole cycle of the body scan practice. This means you have noticed all parts of the body.

- To conclude your body scan, you can now move to the top of the head and stay there for a few seconds.
- Smile at your body. Thank it for being the wonder that it is. Thank it for being your support system and companion and for working so hard to keep you going.
- Smile, breathing mindfully for a few breaths, and then you can end your practice.

This practice will take about fifteen minutes. It may take longer as you become more aware of sensations in your body. If you can regularly find time to do this, you will feel a deep connection with your body over time.

When you notice the body with such kindness and understanding and thank it regularly, it understands that you are choosing to connect with it. It receives your friendliness and feels better. It becomes energetic, heals faster, stays healthier and makes you feel better too.

PRACTICE SUMMARY

Friedrich Nietzsche, a German philosopher known for his work in the area of self-realization, said, 'There is more wisdom in your body than in your deepest philosophy.'

Kabir, in his poem 'Is Ghat Antar', says, the body is our guru.

These are such powerful statements.

In the *Satipatthana Sutta*, an important text containing the Buddha's teachings, he taught the four foundations of mindfulness. The very first one was the mindfulness of the body.

Recently, many psychotherapists and neuroscientists have become keenly aware of the body and its importance in mental health. They have, through research, begun to understand how the mind and body are deeply connected. They have found that having a rested and healthy body is essential to good mental health.

We have only focused on the superficial physical attributes of the body for a long time and ignored the treasure trove of wisdom that it is.

You have now started the process of rediscovering its real beauty by listening to it. Keep listening patiently and lovingly. Check in with your body often. Support it regularly. Stay kind to it and relax it by practising the body scan. Keep your practice regular. It is the best thing you can do for yourself.

Here is a regular practice schedule for you. You can now stop following the routines suggested in Part I and Part II and follow the routines provided below instead.

I am sharing with you three possible routines here. Choose whichever one you feel like following on a particular day. However, make sure you are practising all three routines through the week.

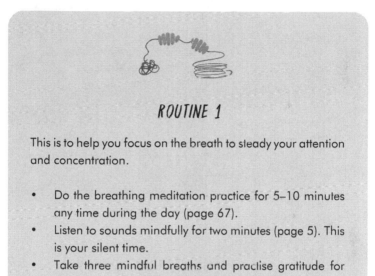

ROUTINE 1

This is to help you focus on the breath to steady your attention and concentration.

- Do the breathing meditation practice for 5–10 minutes any time during the day (page 67).
- Listen to sounds mindfully for two minutes (page 5). This is your silent time.
- Take three mindful breaths and practise gratitude for one minute before you go to sleep (page 42).

ROUTINE 2

This is to help you focus on the body to increase body awareness and relaxation.

- Do the body scan practice (page 115) any time during the day. The days you don't get the space to do the entire body scan practice, do all the one-minute practices for the body (page 110) back to back. Together, these will not take not more than five minutes.
- Be mindful during an entire activity. For instance, eat a fruit/snack mindfully, brush mindfully or bathe mindfully.
- Take three mindful breaths and practise gratitude for one minute before you go to sleep.

ROUTINE 3

This is to help you focus on compassion to increase friendliness and kindness.

- Do the metta practice (page 89) any time during the day.
- Take fifteen mindful breaths and then appreciate yourself for one thing today.
- Take three mindful breaths and practise gratitude for one minute before you go to sleep.

REFLECTION SPACE

PART IV

MAKING FRIENDS
WITH YOUR FEELINGS

1

UNDERSTANDING FEELINGS

Here is a poem I wrote for you to help you understand what making friends with your feelings or emotions can be like.

BEFRIENDING YOUR FEELINGS

My Fear came knocking,
Early one morning
Said My Fear, 'Hi friend!'
'I'm here to tell you how this will end.'
'No one will love you, no matter what you do
'They will laugh at you, and this is true
'You will end up failing, even if you try
'Now, why make a fool of yourself? Oh, why?'

My Anger came next,
Said, 'They are all unfair,
'They deserve your wrath! They made you despair.
'Lash out at them now, speak never to them again,
'Don't let them fool you; they aren't your friends.'
My Sadness came then,
And said, 'You are all alone,
'What a miserable life, when you have no one.
'You're neither good at stuff, nor have what
you want,
'You will never be fun. You know you just can't!
'Your friends on Insta, they are doing so well.
'Your life is just pointless; it seems like hell.'

I heard them out, fearful, angry and sad,
I watched them with all the compassion I had.
I knew these were tales of a fearful mind,
I stayed gentle, I remained kind.
And as I watched, they slowly eased,
The distress had now changed to peace.
Then I could hear, the quiet voice inside
Speaking to me as a friend and a guide
It's message was simple, it said, 'Just be.
'You're already happy. You're already free.'

This poem expresses how our feelings and the stories our minds spin, appear as one. But they are not actually as intertwined as they seem to be. It is possible to watch our emotions with understanding and love without believing the stories associated with them. Not only is this possible but there is also great benefit in befriending our feelings in this way. Our emotions and feelings carry wise messages for our well-being. We will practise understanding and working with our feelings in this section of the book.

Our feelings and emotions are an essential part of us. Sometimes we might be able to identify how we are feeling, but we barely know how to be friendly towards our feelings or emotions. In fact, most of the time we just want the uncomfortable feelings to go away.

For instance, we may feel hurt or sad, but do we know how to be friendly towards the pain or the sadness? Not really. In fact, it seems like such a strange notion to be friendly towards pain or sadness, doesn't it? Nevertheless, it is very much possible to create some friendliness towards all our feelings.

But before we can make friends with our feelings, we have to understand them better. To make it easier for you, the words 'feelings' and 'emotions' have been used interchangeably.

What Are Feelings? How Do We Experience Them?

Let us take an example to understand feelings and emotions better.

Suma is walking in the school corridor when she trips on the carpet and falls on her hands. A group of kids standing around start laughing at her. What does Suma feel? She feels embarrassed and highly self-conscious. She wants to quickly get away from there. In this situation, it might be easy for us to guess how she might be feeling. However, let us examine what might be happening below the surface, behind what meets our eyes.

Suma tripped and fell down. She felt a bit of fear while falling because she lost her balance. Then as soon as she gained control, she realized people were staring and laughing at her. A thought came to her: 'They must be thinking I am so clumsy'. Her mind created a thought of judgement.

Simultaneously, a lot was happening in her body too. Her face appeared flushed. Her heart was pumping fast, and her legs wanted to move quickly and take her away from this difficult situation.

At an emotional level, she felt embarrassed, and at a behavioural level, she wanted to run away from the situation and probably wished she could hide for a bit!

Similarly, when we go through intense emotion, we too have so many things happening within us at the same time. But we are rarely aware of them. This is because we are not very mindful of what is going on within us at all.

As seen in Part II, our mind quickly gets into the storytelling mode. Then we ignore our body and feelings completely. If we need to understand and make friends with difficult feelings like embarrassment, sadness, jealousy and anger, we need to start observing them closely while also knowing what is happening in our mind and body when we are feeling this particular way.

2

OUR USUAL WAY OF DEALING WITH FEELINGS

We, typically, have developed three habitual and unhealthy ways of dealing with feelings:

- We try to push the feeling away.
- We start overthinking and try to think our way out of feeling.
- We get caught in the 'storm' of the emotions and give in to them by reacting.

Neither of these ways are helpful. We will use Samar's example to better understand these unhelpful ways of dealing with feelings.

Samar is a fourteen-year-old boy and has a brother who is a few years younger than him. While Samar is a quiet child, focused on studies, his younger brother is an extrovert. He is talkative and charms people. As he is small, cute and talkative, the younger brother gets a lot of attention. Samar feels alone and neglected by his family and the visitors who come to their home.

Samar does not realize what he is feeling. He is probably jealous of his brother, angry at him, and maybe also sad. He is jealous and angry at his brother for always being the centre of attention and sad because he feels left out and lonely. But Samar is not aware of all these different feelings. He only knows that he feels upset when visitors come over to his place.

1. Dealing with feelings by pushing them away

The first unhealthy way in which we deal with feelings is by pushing them away.

If Samar were to deal with his emotions by pushing them away, he would do things to avoid feeling anything. Perhaps he would avoid his younger brother, especially when visitors came over. He might stay in his own room, not wanting to meet anyone, and distract himself by playing games on his phone.

But by doing so, Samar is not recognizing how he feels. He is dealing with the difficult feelings by pushing them away and distracting himself through games. Is this helping him, though?

For the time being, maybe it helps him. Instead of feeling upset, playing games keeps him distracted. But the feeling does not go away. It comes back each time the situation repeats itself, whenever visitors come home. In fact, over time, he only dreads the situation more. He increasingly feels more and more upset and trapped.

Have you heard of the phrase 'Sweeping dirt under the rug'? It means that when the house is dirty, instead of cleaning it up, we just push the dirt under a rug. What will happen if we keep doing this? The house will appear clean, but we are only concealing the dirt; it's still there. Then maybe some insects or worms will breed in the dirt. It will never get clean on its own by avoiding looking at the dirt. In fact, it will only get worse.

So, if we really need to clean our house, we have to do two things. First, we have to stop pushing more dirt under the rug, and second, we have to lift the rug, confront all the dirt that has collected so far and start cleaning it up.

Dealing with feelings by pushing them away is like sweeping dirt under the rug. This is the first type of mistake we often make. Instead of paying attention to our feelings and acknowledging them, we push them away. Our feelings don't go away just because we do not take notice of them. They stay right where they are, and they get worse.

Samar, for instance, is not going to suddenly start feeling better one day, as nothing has been done to understand his feelings and to make friends with them.

What we, therefore, need to do is to start observing our feelings carefully and try to understand them and support ourselves. We will learn how to do that in a bit. For now, let us see the other unhealthy ways of dealing with feelings.

2. Dealing with feelings by overthinking

The second type of mistake we make is dealing with feelings by overthinking. Instead of acknowledging and trying to understand the emotion or feeling, we get involved in the stories our mind is making.

In Samar's situation, if he was caught up in his mind's stories, he could think his brother was a terrible attention-seeker or that he was a fake person putting up a show for other people. He could create many such judgements against his brother. Or he could conclude that he is not good enough to be liked by others. He might even develop low self-esteem by thinking that he will never be good enough and that people won't find him interesting.

Again, these are stories created by his mind and are not reflective of the truth. We have spent quite a bit of time understanding this earlier (page 70). As we can see, overthinking does not get Samar any closer to understanding his feelings or helping him through the difficult emotions he experiences.

3. Dealing with feelings by getting reactive

The third unhealthy way of dealing with feelings is by becoming reactive and agitated.

If Samar were to deal with his feelings by getting reactive, he would express his anger loudly. He may verbally criticize his brother, or even throw a tantrum in front of his parents or the visitors.

Though on the face of it, it might appear that he is letting himself be emotional, in truth, he would still not be able to understand his genuine feelings or stay with them, leave alone making friends with them. This method, of instantly showing his displeasure by reacting, might temporarily make him feel better since he has had the opportunity to express, lash out and show his anger. But the anger will drain him, and upset him deeply too. It will also, possibly, make him feel lonely and abandoned in the long run as others might avoid him due to his aggressive behaviour. Perhaps his parents could also over time begin to feel helpless in the face of his tantrums, and they may appear disappointed with him.

As we can see, neither of the above three habitual or regular ways of dealing with feelings and emotions is helpful. Neither of these ways provide any real insight into the feelings. Also, none of them seem to reduce unhappiness in the long run. They are merely temporary fixes and unwise methods of approaching our deep emotions.

However, it is understandable that we would relate to our feelings in these ways because we just don't know any other way. We learnt so many things in school, but no one ever taught us how to work with our feelings or address our emotions. So we learnt by watching others, who very likely also dealt with their emotions in unhealthy ways.

The wise sages and enlightened beings, however, studied their mind, body and feelings very deeply. They spent years in meditation, in going within and making sense of their inner world.

Thanks to them, we have some wonderful ways available to us to deal with our feelings with wisdom. These are methods that may seem difficult or heavy at the outset, but they are paths to a joyful, empowered and peaceful life.

Before we go on to learn how to work wisely with feelings, let's do an exercise to understand how you currently deal with your feelings.

EXERCISE: HOW DO YOU DEAL WITH YOUR FEELINGS?

Put down examples of one current or long-standing situation that creates difficult feelings in you.

Example: My mom always praises my other friends in front of me, but she does not say anything good about me in front of others.

Now write about your situation here:

_____

_____

_____

_____

What are the feelings this situation brings up? Put down your feelings below.

Example: I feel hurt and rejected when my mom does that.

_____

_____

_____

_____

How do you deal with these feelings? Do you push them away, do you get into overthinking mode or do you quickly react?

Example of pushing feelings away: I feel terrible and just leave the room when she is praising other people and try to put my mind to something else.

OR

Example of overthinking: 'Why can my mom not see the good things about me? Will she ever think I am good? She always does this. She did it the last time too when I was playing football. I am working so hard at learning it, but she only praised my teammate.

OR

Example of reacting: I get so irritated with my mom that I shout at her, criticize her and tell her she is not a good mother and compare her to my friends' mothers. Or I throw a tantrum on some other small unrelated issue to vent my frustration.

Use the space below to write what you really do to deal with your feelings.

_____

_____

_____

_____

Now that we have thought through our situation, the feelings it brings up, and we know a little more about how we deal with it, let us learn a different and wise way of dealing with feelings, especially the difficult ones.

3

A WISE WAY OF WORKING WITH DIFFICULT FEELINGS

Four Steps to Working with Difficult Feelings

Here is a super-short rhyme, I want you to commit to memory. This is going to help you a lot when you go through an intense emotion or a difficult feeling.

I Pause when I feel it
I Name it, Accept it, Support it.

This rhyme contains the four steps you need to deal with difficult emotions. Let us understand each step and how to go about it, and then we can practise.

Step 1: Pause (when you feel it)
Step 2: Name it
Step 3: Accept it
Step 4: Support it

Step 1: Pause

When you recognize you are feeling uneasy or when a difficult feeling starts to appear, the first thing to do is pause. Before you do anything, just wait and slow down. Take a few deep breaths.

Here is how to breathe while pausing: Take slow deep breaths that fill up your belly. As you breathe in, let your belly inflate like a balloon. As you breathe out, let your belly deflate. Do this for 7–10 breaths.

This pause is needed to create a space between the feeling and our habitual way of dealing with it, whether it is by pushing it away or getting caught up in stories or reacting.

To pause, you can try finding a relatively quiet space in your surroundings. A place you can be alone in for some time. If that is not possible (in an examination hall, for example), just take a few deep breaths mindfully in the same place and create that space internally within you.

Step 2: Name it

A common saying in the world of feelings is, 'Name it to tame it.' Let's understand what that means.

Often, a feeling is something vague. We know that the feeling is 'unpleasant' or 'uneasy', but we do not clearly know what it is. Is it sadness, jealousy, anger or loneliness?

In fact, we rarely even ask ourselves, 'What am I actually feeling?'

Naming our feelings is a very important step in dealing with them effectively. For one, only when we are able to name our feelings can we know what we need to do to help ourselves. Also, research has shown that naming the feeling reduces the intensity of the emotion and provides a little relief.

How can one recognize and name their feelings?

After you have taken a pause, which is the first step, ask yourself, 'What am I feeling now?'

Stay patient and quiet for your intuition to awaken. If you feel lost, ask yourself a broad question, 'Am I feeling glad, sad, angry or afraid?' You will know which way you are leaning towards.

You can also take the help of your body to understand your feelings. Remember that the body speaks in the language of sensations. Through sensations, it can tell us what we are feeling—we only need to listen. Sometimes, it knows what we are feeling even before our thinking mind knows. To become adept at the language of sensations, you must continue your body scan practice. Then you will know your sensations better and they will help you recognize your feelings.

For example, your stomach may feel uneasy just before an exam because you are tense or nervous. Sometimes, your face may become hot when you are angry, or your jaws may become tight because you are trying to control an angry outburst. In these cases, sensations may be quite clear.

Sometimes, the language of sensations is not very clear. For instance, 'heaviness' in the chest, 'a knot-like feeling' in the stomach, 'weakness' in the knees are sensations that do not directly tell us what feeling is present. Yet, they are still useful to name and become aware of.

In such a situation, to name the feeling, you have to gently ask yourself, 'What am I feeling now?' and then quietly notice the body sensations. Simply accept whatever answer comes up through your intuition. Usually, if we have been successful in naming the emotion, there is a little more ease or some letting go that is experienced.

Now onwards, start noticing your body sensations every time you feel a strong feeling or emotion. With practice, you will get better at using body sensations to name feelings. They will become your cues to know what's going on inside you. For example, a hollowness in the stomach might help you know that you are feeling insecure, or a flushed face might be a cue of feeling embarrassed.

If you still feel confused, take the help of the checklist below. It contains names of common emotions and feelings. Read them and ask yourself patiently which feeling are you most likely experiencing now. The word 'now' is important. You want to notice only what you are feeling in the present. You are trying to know the emotion that is present right at this moment, not something that you usually experience or that you experienced earlier. Remember, this is a way of being with yourself in the present, mindfully.

CHECKLIST OF FEELINGS AND EMOTIONS

PLEASANT FEELINGS	DIFFICULT/UNPLEASANT FEELINGS
Glad	Ashamed
Joyful	Irritated
Appreciated	Hurt
Satisfied	Lonely
Loved	Unloved
Enthusiastic	Angry
Cheerful	Confused
Grateful	Embarrassed
Relaxed	Jealous
Peaceful	Disappointed

Use this checklist to help you identify the feeling arising in you. For instance, when someone has a gadget or dress that you have been wanting, or when someone else is getting attention, or when a friend is mean to you, what is it that you feel in that moment? Anger, jealousy, hurt? Just recognize it and name it.

Step 3: Accept it

Accepting our feelings is the most important of all the steps. All our feelings are okay! Yes, any feeling we have is valid. It is okay to feel jealous, angry, sad or afraid. In fact, it is totally natural and normal to experience these feelings.

I know, our parents and teachers repeatedly tell us to not be jealous or scared. What they actually mean is that we must not take jealousy or fear too seriously. We all get jealous, afraid, angry and disappointed from time to time. It is only human to experience difficult emotions.

So having difficult feelings and emotions is not the problem. Taking them too seriously and not wanting to feel anything unpleasant, is the bigger problem.

We treat difficult feelings like they are a bad thing. We don't want them. When we are sad, we don't want to be sad. When we are anxious, we don't want to be anxious. We don't want these feelings because they are so unpleasant, and that is understandable. But we also have to understand our feelings are parts of us. If we reject them, we are rejecting parts of ourselves. Can we ever be happy rejecting ourselves?

Feelings are also impermanent, like thoughts, like everything else. They come and go. They arise and pass away. They don't stay forever. And they especially don't last long if we don't build stories around them, making them bigger than they are.

In fact, there is a saying: 'What you resist persists'. So, ignoring our emotions actually prolongs their existence.

For instance, if you are feeling jealous, simply tell yourself, 'Yes, I am feeling jealous right now, and it is okay.' This is the simple truth. There is nothing right or wrong about it. It is just a feeling, and in some time, it will pass.

The very fact that you have accepted it, will lighten your uneasiness. You are no longer resisting feeling jealous. You are accepting it as a reality of this moment.

You can say to yourself, 'Yes, it feels uneasy now, but I can stay with it and wait until it passes.' Meanwhile, you can practise staying present, noticing your breath and body sensations. You can also try to support your feelings, in a friendly way, which is the next step.

Step 4: Support it

So far you have gone through the first three steps. You have paused, named your feeling and accepted it. Most of the tough work is over. Now the fourth step is like a soothing balm. This step will bring gentleness, friendliness and kindness to dealing with emotions. In this step, you will support your feelings.

To 'support' means to extend a kind understanding towards something or someone. When your friends are upset, how do you support them? You support them by saying kind words. You say 'I understand you', 'Do not worry', 'It will be okay.' Or you do something to make them feel better. Perhaps you put a hand on their shoulder to show you are with them. This is the kind of support you can give yourself too.

How can you give yourself such support? You can use supportive statements like, 'I am angry because I am hurt, I am going to care for myself', 'I am jealous because I feel insecure,

I will be kind to myself' or 'I am lonely right now, I need my own love, I am going to try to love myself through this lonely feeling'.

Then you can go one step further and support yourself physically. If you have been practising mindfulness of the body regularly, you can notice how your body feels right now.

For instance, if you feel very anxious, your body will feel tense and anxious too, and you can notice this. Your stomach may feel like it's in knots, your shoulders may feel tight, and your heart may beat a bit faster. You can support yourself by easing your shoulders or by gently keeping a hand on your belly or chest in a supportive way. You can also take deep breaths if that feels supportive. Deep breaths can slow down your heartbeat and calm you down.

Support can also involve moving your body gently and slowly, especially if it is getting tight or stiff due to the emotion. For example, you can move your jaws slowly when you feel tightness in them or you can move your neck a little when it feels stiff. I have explained this way of supporting the body in Part III (page 113).

The emotion may feel overwhelming and you may feel the need to lie down or sit or even slowly walk around the room. Feel free to rest and support your body as it is asking to be supported.

When you listen to your body, allow it to do what it needs, and it will ease and open up. This really helps your feelings to get lighter and your mind to get clearer. It is important to give yourself time to tune in, listen and then take the time to do what the body needs.

In Part V of the book, I have elaborated on how to work with many different emotions. However, across all emotions, the same four steps of pausing, naming, accepting and supporting are applicable.

Let us practise these four steps now so that you are familiar with them, even though you may not be necessarily going through a difficult feeling at the moment.

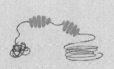

PRACTICE: FOUR STEPS TO WORKING WITH DIFFICULT FEELINGS

Pause: Start the practice with pausing for a few breaths. Breathe deeply, letting your belly inflate with each breath. Stay mindful of your breathing throughout.

Name it: Ask yourself how you are feeling now. Ask your body how it is feeling now. Let the answer come from within you without overthinking it. Let your body answer. If there is no difficult emotion right now, maybe you are feeling calm or neutral. Just tell yourself, 'I am feeling calm or neutral.'

(When you come back to this practice while experiencing an intense emotion, check in to see what you are feeling then. If the feeling is vague and you are unable to put a name to it, consult the checklist given on page 139. With practise, you will get better at naming your emotions.)

Accept it: Now tell yourself, 'I am okay with whatever I am feeling now. My feeling is welcome.' If it is a calm feeling, just enjoy it. If it is a difficult feeling, try to accept it, knowing it is temporary and will pass.

Support it: Ease your body a bit if it is uneasy with the feeling. Notice your body sensations and support them. Put a hand on your chest to support yourself. Say to yourself, 'I will try to be kind towards what I am feeling. Whether the feeling is pleasant or unpleasant, I will support it.' Now sit with it as long as you like or is possible. Once you have sat with your feelings for a while, you can get back to whatever you need to do.

If you practise listening to your feelings and emotions with such kindness, support and acceptance, you will slowly develop a very loving and friendly relationship with yourself. You will become happier and more peaceful with time.

4

THE IMPORTANCE OF NOTICING PLEASANT FEELINGS

We have, in detail, gone through working with difficult emotions. However, should only difficult emotions be noticed? While we are most uneasy with the difficult emotions and therefore most motivated to ease them, our pleasant and comfortable emotions are as important to notice. When we feel warm, friendly, cosy and happy, we would benefit greatly by pausing and naming those emotions too.

When we notice pleasant emotions and feel them in our bodies, our brain reduces its inherent or ingrained negativity bias (page 79). Our brain learns to recognize that things are going well too. We can then learn to stay aware of the pleasant emotion and enjoy it while it lasts.

We also become more realistic. We become aware that both pleasant and difficult emotions visit us. Both are only visitors. They come and go. Nothing lasts. They are all impermanent.

We realize that we can be welcoming and kind to all emotions and body sensations without judging them or making stories about them. We understand that nature will make us feel both sad and happy, comfortable and uncomfortable.

When we develop such a wise acceptance and allowance for all emotions and feelings to visit us, we truly become a wonderful friend to ourselves.

PRACTICE SUMMARY

'Pain is inevitable. Suffering is optional'—this is a profound quote, attributed to several different people.

While going through this part on feelings, we have clearly seen that we cannot help the painful, unpleasant situations and the resulting difficult feelings that arise. However, we can definitely suffer less if we befriend our feelings in a wise and aware way.

The challenge in the area of mindfulness is that while we understand the concepts, and are even convinced about them, we cannot fully apply them to our life unless we internalize them.

Mindfulness is internalized when it becomes our natural response. When we are naturally mindful, we recognize quite soon that our mind has wandered away and are quick to bring our attention back into the present. We are aware of feeling emotional and of how that is reflecting in our body. We become instantly aware that we are judging ourselves or others and we are able to move towards a more compassionate outlook. If we internalize mindfulness like this, our joyfulness will tremendously increase. This can, however, only happen when we regularly reflect on the concepts and we stay regular with our practice.

So here is how you can practise going forward:

- You can continue to work with one of the three routines laid out in Part III (pages 119–20), as they include the three main practices of breathing meditation, body scan and metta. They also include a short gratitude practice. It is important that you cover all three different routines on different days. If you practise these regularly, you will find that life will start to become more manageable and peaceful for you—and I can confidently say this to you due to my own experience with these practices.

- In addition to the above routines, if and when you go through any difficult feelings or emotions, please do the practice explained on pages 143–44. It is to be done when you really need help with your emotions, which is often enough. Also, remember to keep noticing and appreciating the times when pleasant feelings arise in you.

REFLECTION SPACE

PART V

DEALING WITH SPECIFIC EMOTIONS AND DIFFICULT SITUATIONS

Congratulations! You have been through a long and meaningful journey through the pages of this book.

The previous four sections on making friends with yourself, your mind, your body and your feelings have already provided you with an abundance of concepts and practices to use in various situations.

In this section, I have chosen specific difficulties that your age group has to contend with regularly. I have tried to explain in detail how to manage these emotions and situations when they arise in your life. So in order to apply the learnings from the previous sections, it is important that you understand them before getting started with this one.

1

DEALING WITH ANGER

Your attempt to be here, to try to understand your anger and make friends with it, is praiseworthy. Most people get frustrated and vent their anger on others and just accept that that's what one does when one is angry. Others shut it down by trying not to feel it and become quite bitter over time.

Anger is no easy emotion to manage. One reason is that it feels so explosive inside. We feel like punching something and yelling at someone. We just find it all so unbearable, and it's hard to know what to do.

Yet, anger is such a common emotion. All of us feel angry at some point or the other. If we make an effort to understand our anger better, we can deal with it in a way that is more helpful to us and less harmful to others.

Understanding Anger Clearly

1. We get angry because we want things to be in our control and they are not

Anger and control have a very close relationship. We want to control things, which means we want life to be as we *expect*. We wish that things happen as we think they should. Life, however, does not always work according to our wishes. Sometimes we do not get what we want. At times, someone else gets what we want. Sometimes people disagree with us, say things that are unkind and even tease us.

We cannot control what is happening around us. Such is life. No one has much control over life. Since we don't realize this fundamental fact, we get more frustrated and angry when things do not go our way.

Next time you feel angry, check to see if you're feeling that things are going out of your control.

2. There are often different feelings underlying our anger

So for instance, you want to go outside and play or hang out with your friends, but your parents have grounded you for not completing some work. Now, you are restless and bored. You don't want to do what you have to, and instead, you want something else, which is getting out of the house and being with your friends. So, you become angry at your parents. Maybe you throw a tantrum or yell and scream.

You see, in this case, your anger is actually arising from being bored and having lots of pent-up energy.

Here is another example. Let's say your friend made fun of you at school. You feel angry with her. Underneath the anger, though, you are hurt. You feel betrayed. How could your friend be so mean to you? However, you are more aware of the anger than of the hurt.

As you can see, some deeper emotion is often hiding behind our anger.

This is just for your understanding. I am not asking you to identify the underlying emotion. That could be difficult. However, as you get better at listening to your body and emotions and checking how you feel, the real emotion will become apparent.

3. We believe people want to hurt us knowingly

When we are angry at people, it is because we believe people who are nasty to us are being so on purpose. We accept that we cannot fully control our minds, but we assume that others who are hurting us have complete control over theirs! This is faulty thinking.

Like us, the people who harm us are also caught up in their minds' storytelling, intense emotions, unpleasant body sensations or difficult life situations. They cause harm to us because they don't know how to handle their feelings.

Since you have been working with your body and emotions, you recognize that it is not easy to understand your mind and manage your feelings. It takes the right perspective as well as regular effort. Most people have either not come across this knowledge, haven't understood it fully or haven't practised it.

When intense emotions like anger or fear overtake them, they do not know what to do—just like us. They become agitated and try to manage it by directing it towards others, creating violence and hurting others.

Often, the reason for war and violence in the world is that people don't understand themselves or know their real feelings and why they are attacking others. They don't realize that they are caught up in the endless cycle of dukkha and suffering and that violence will eventually only make them feel worse.

So you see, the people who cause harm to us are themselves not feeling great. What is the point then of spending our energy in blaming them?

Happy people do not hurt others. Only those suffering and unhappy from within judge and cause harm to others. So, when people hurt us, if we realize that they are also suffering somehow, our anger might ease a bit.

When we work with our own feelings, we learn to see others as not intentionally evil or mean, but as people who are lost and don't know how to handle their own emotions.

There is a beautiful quote attributed to the Buddha. It says, 'Holding on to anger is like grasping a hot coal with the intent of throwing it at someone else; you are the one who gets burnt.'

Let us understand anger with the help of an example.

Mishti and Teresa were close friends in the ninth grade. Mishti had developed a crush on a new classmate who had joined school that year. It was, of course, a secret and no one else knew about it. One day, she confided in Teresa and asked her to keep it to herself and not tell anyone about it.

However, when Teresa was chatting with another classmate, she gave in to the temptation to discuss Mishti's crush. After that, one person told another, and soon, everyone in the class was talking about it. The person she had a crush on, also heard about it and became very awkward around Mishti.

Going to school became very uncomfortable and embarrassing for her. She was so angry with Teresa that she refused to look at her or speak to her. She had constant angry thoughts about how Teresa had broken her trust: *Teresa is the worst and most untrustworthy person ever. She is not even my friend! She purposely hurt me. I will never speak to her again.*

She also had thoughts of blaming herself for confiding in Teresa. *I should have never told her. I was a fool to have trusted her. I am not going to trust anyone with my secrets ever again.*

We can understand that this situation is very hard on Mishti. She has lost a friend in Teresa, is embarrassed at having her secret known to all, has been distanced from her crush, and is now feeling lonely and blaming herself too. What an uneasy feeling. And so much anger.

On the other hand, it is not as though Teresa is entirely unaffected. Teresa has also lost out on a friend. She was tempted to gossip with one person, but she may not have known she was going to cause so much damage.

Also, if we try to understand Teresa's mind, we will see that gossiping about her friend was giving in to a weakness. Maybe she felt important carrying juicy news and was unable to overcome that temptation. Her mind had overpowered her. She did not necessarily want to hurt Mishti.

And yet Mishti was really hurt.

People may or may not intend to hurt us so much. They may act out of their weakness, habit, temptation or from some fabricated mind story, but we do get hurt. Then we feel angry, helpless and out of control.

Mishti's example is of anger that is associated with a recent situation. However, at times, our anger can be very old. Somebody could have hurt us badly in the past or perhaps continues to do so. We may feel angry with a parent, sibling, teacher or someone who was close to us and harmed us somehow.

If we don't address our old anger, we will slowly become very bitter about that person. It is important to stay aware that we may hold such old anger in us as well.

Dealing with Anger Wisely

Whether our anger is in reaction to something that is happening now or it is anger from the past, the first thing we need to do is be kind to ourselves. Yes, that is right! If we are feeling angry, then deep down we must be hurt, sad or in some kind of emotional pain. We have to direct our attention, kindness and love towards ourselves first because this pain needs comforting.

Thich Nhat Hanh, a Vietnamese Buddhist monk and a revered teacher, has a kind and compassionate way of dealing with life that has inspired me a great deal. He teaches a wise and gentle way of working with anger and suggests that we think of our anger like a flower bud that is closed at the moment. He asks us to expose it to the sunshine of our love and compassion regularly. In time, it will open up and our anger will ease. What a gentle and beautiful analogy, comparing anger to a flower!

To give ourselves love and compassion, we need to turn our attention towards ourselves and away from the person or situation that is provoking our anger. By shifting focus in this way, we are also letting go of our mind's stories about the situation or person who is making us angry.

Now that our attention is here, in the present, and focused on our emotion, we apply the same method of dealing with feelings that we learnt earlier.

Let's revisit the rhyme:

> I Pause when I feel it,
> I Name it, Accept it, Support it.

Now, follow these four steps:

Step 1: Pause

When you feel anger, recognize what your habitual pattern of dealing with it is. Do you feel like shutting it down by distracting yourself? Are you getting caught up in overthinking? Do you feel like reacting?

Revisiting the practice you did earlier to recognize your way of dealing with feelings will help (pages 143–44). Instead of giving in to your habitual tendency, try to pause.

Take a few deep breaths. Feel the breaths in your belly. Rest your attention on the rising and falling of your abdomen.

Step 2: Name it

You already have a name for your emotion. You know you are feeling angry. Tell yourself, 'I am angry now. I will simply spend some time knowing my anger.' Promise yourself that you will decide what to do with the person or situation later. For now, you will simply attend to this feeling of anger.

This is not the time for thoughts, stories or even trying to find a solution. During an intense emotion, the rational part of our brain stops working well. Hence, it is least helpful to try and find solutions or fix problems at such a time.

Step 3: Accept it

That you are angry is the reality of the present moment. As we have understood earlier, it is always okay to feel any feeling. It is okay to feel angry for now. There is no question about whether you should or should not feel angry.

Instead, just simply accepting it will suffice. Maybe you can say to yourself, 'I am angry now, and it is okay.'

Step 4: Support it

Remind yourself that you need your own affection and support now. Anger is such a difficult feeling, so painful to go through.

Do a quick body scan. Notice where you might feel anger in your body. Here are some of the ways you may feel anger in your body. Check to see if you relate with any of these:

- You may feel anger in your jaws. There may be tightness there.
- You may feel it in the form of heat in your face or elsewhere in your body.
- Anger is usually a high-energy emotion. You may feel like moving your arms or legs to express anger.

You may also feel it in many other ways. Accept all the sensations in the body completely.

Now that you can sense what the body is going through, you can actively support it. Support means allowing the body to feel the anger and helping it through a difficult time. It does not mean trying to stop being angry.

Here are two effective ways to support yourself through anger:

1. Make supportive movements

You can make some movements to help your body deal with anger. These movements require you to really listen to your body. What does your body want to do now? How does it want to move? Move it the way that feels intuitively right for you. Keep the movements gentle and slow, though. You want to give your body ample time and space to feel the effects of the movement.

Since anger is a high-energy emotion, allowing your arms and legs to move may help. You could make some slow marching movements in one place. You can also stretch your legs and kick them out a few times very slowly.

You can use your arms to make pushing movements towards the front or the side or upwards. This will help ease the tension in your arms.

You can move your jaws, loosen them a little. Make slow biting movements with your mouth.

Repeatedly remind yourself to keep your movements slow and mindful. Do them to create support for the overwhelming feeling of anger.

2. Use touch as support

Now, once you make these supportive movements, sit down in a relaxed manner. Preferably sit in a comfortable chair unless your body feels like lying down. If it does, feel free to lie down. Remember, support means listening to the body and helping it to relax. Always listen to the body and your intuition.

Now, take some deep breaths. Check where you can place a hand on your body to help it feel supported. Just to explore, keep your hand on your chest. Take a few seconds to sense how that feels inside your chest. See if that feels supportive. Check whether you need to adjust the support a bit. Do you feel like moving your hand higher or lower or changing the pressure of your touch? Go ahead and do whatever feels right.

Similarly, you could explore by keeping a hand on your belly, on the top of your head or on your forehead. You might even want to just hold yourself in a hug by wrapping your arms around your body.

Each time you support yourself through touch, stay that way to feel the support deeply for a few seconds. If a touch feels comforting, stay with it for as long as you like. Don't be in a hurry. Only when you take in support deeply will your emotions respond and soften.

Remind yourself that you are only angry because something upset you, and in some time, the feeling will pass away. No one stays angry forever. It may return, but each time it does, you have the steps to work with it wisely and in a friendly way.

If you work with anger like this when it arises and continue to practise meditation regularly, your anger will become less intense and difficult over time.

2

DEALING WITH BOREDOM

How often have you said or felt that you are bored? I am sure many times! But have you ever stopped to check what it means to feel bored? Or what happens in your mind and body when you feel bored? In this section, we are going to try to understand and learn to manage boredom by being mindful of it.

How Do You Manage Your Boredom?

What do you typically do when boredom visits you? Here are some ways that you might usually deal with boredom:

1. You may complain to your parents or friends. You may say, 'I am boooooored' in a long drawl and feel irritable. They may then suggest some options to you that you may or may not like.
2. You may distract yourself by switching on the TV, listening to music, playing games or checking social media if you are old enough to do that. Sometimes, even when you don't want to do these activities, you keep doing them because you are bored.
3. You may call or text your friends.

None of these methods by themselves is a problem, but they do point to something interesting about *you*. They show you that you do not know how to rest with yourself when there is nothing to do. You do not know how to enjoy your own company. In fact, you might never even have tried to be in your own company in a relaxed way, without having something to do.

People your age are not the only ones who do not know how to rest with themselves. Most adults are the same. They also do not know how to relax in their own company. Instead, they choose to distract themselves by repeatedly checking their social media, chatting with friends or sometimes even getting addicted to smoking or drinking. All this to avoid feeling restless and bored.

Most human beings have not been taught how to simply rest by themselves without getting distracted or hooked on to something.

Blaise Pascal, a seventeenth-century French mathematician and philosopher said, 'All men's miseries derive from not being able to sit in a quiet room alone.'

This quote nails it! If you cannot sit with yourself quietly, you are bound to have more misery and unhappiness.

Boredom Is a Great Teacher

I know it sounds strange, but boredom is a great teacher. It prepares us for one crucial fact about life: that life is not meant to be about having one entertainment after another.

Many adults who have not understood this get used to keeping themselves busy by working or entertaining themselves constantly. They have not developed the habit of resting and enjoying their own company and hence believe they must constantly be doing something. The result is that they accumulate a lot of stress over time as their system gets no downtime.

You are growing up in the same world. If you do not understand boredom and practise staying with it, you too will try to be constantly entertained. You are probably already doing that now—craving episode after episode of your favourite series or eating mindlessly to distract yourself, unable to tolerate getting bored.

However, as I said earlier, life is not meant to be constantly entertaining. It is filled with neutral moments where you are just in a routine. Moments where you are brushing, bathing, eating, walking, talking and so on. So, if you find life uninteresting sometimes, it is most natural and understandable. It is how it is meant to be. And it is perfectly okay.

So, our first step in dealing with boredom is accepting that it is okay to be bored sometimes. Boredom is just a part of life. Everyone gets bored. At times, it may even be good to be bored because then we have the opportunity to practise being quiet with ourselves, becoming our own friend.

Boredom also teaches us to be creative and spontaneous. Creative people like artists, film-makers and writers purposely put themselves in situations where there are few people, lots of quiet time and very little to do. They use the lack of entertainment or external distractions to express themselves creatively.

The Practice of Staying Restfully by Yourself

Now that we have accepted that it is okay to be bored, let's start observing what happens when you are bored.

- **On a thought level:** When you are bored, you may think that you have nothing interesting, exciting or enjoyable to do.
- **On a body level:** You may feel a sense of restlessness. If you check in with your body sensations, you may find a sense of unpleasantness in your body.
- **On a feeling level:** You may start to feel upset and irritated that you do not have any entertainment.

So here is a practice you can do every time you feel bored.

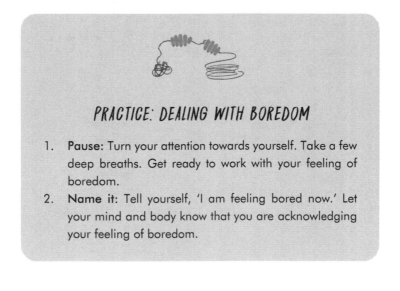

PRACTICE: DEALING WITH BOREDOM

1. **Pause:** Turn your attention towards yourself. Take a few deep breaths. Get ready to work with your feeling of boredom.
2. **Name it:** Tell yourself, 'I am feeling bored now.' Let your mind and body know that you are acknowledging your feeling of boredom.

3. **Accept it:** Remind yourself that it is okay and most natural and normal to feel bored. Everyone feels it. Also, accept that it is not an easy feeling to stay with. It is not pleasant, yet you are trying to stay with it without immediately trying to distract yourself.
4. **Support it:** Now, you can simply support feeling bored by telling yourself that you will use this time to be friends with yourself. You will just relax for some time and notice all the things that you can see around you. You can also notice the laziness or restlessness in the body.

You can use the statements given below to accept and support yourself too while noticing your breath mindfully.

While breathing in, mentally say, 'Breathing in, I know I am bored.'

While breathing out, say, 'Breathing out, I know it is okay to be bored.'

Sometimes when staying steady in our practice is difficult, we can use such phrases to help us stay mindful.

Supporting the body through movement

Notice how your body wants to move. Do you need to stretch or bend? Make the movements your body needs you to make.

Here are some movements involving opening up the joints in your arms and legs, which are particularly helpful in dealing with the restlessness and underlying boredom.

1. Opening up the joints of the legs

Sit comfortably in a chair with your feet on the floor. Lift one foot off the floor, and ever so gently, rotate the ankle in one direction a few times and then in the other direction. You will notice as you do this that your breath will also start to slow down.

Next, work with the knee joint of the same leg. While staying seated, put your hands underneath your thigh as if holding it up from the chair by a few inches. Then slowly swing your leg back and forth a few times. After that, proceed to draw an imaginary number '0' with your foot. This will rotate the knee joint in a circular manner. Do this in a clockwise and anticlockwise direction.

After this, work with the hip joint of the same leg. Bring your knee towards your chest, and then slowly swing it downwards towards the floor. This movement would open up your hip joint. If it doesn't, you can stand up and move your leg forward and backward to open up your hips too.

Repeat the same actions on the other leg in the order of the ankle, knee and hip.

2. Opening up the joints of the arms

When working with the arms, start with the wrist. You can do one arm at a time or both together—whatever feels manageable to you. Rotate the wrists slowly in a clockwise and anticlockwise direction.

After this, move on to the elbow joint. Hold your arms out in front of you. Then move your hands towards your shoulders a few times. The purpose is to move your elbow joint.

Next, work on opening up your shoulder joint. Touch the top of your shoulder with the fingers of the same hand. Now slowly and gently, rotate the shoulders in one direction and then the other.

After these exercises, it is likely that you will feel more relaxed.

Ask your body what it needs now. You can lie down and relax further. After some time, you can end this practice and get back to your routine.

Remember, when we are mindful, we reject neither our boredom, anger or jealousy nor any part of ourselves.

The beauty of mindfulness is that we can arrive at it from so many places. We can check in with our feeling, our body, give ourselves support, or just breathe and rest.

If you spend some time noticing the boredom and making friends with yourself every time you are bored, you will completely change how you feel about being bored.

When you stay with boredom kindly and gently in the way we have just discussed, you will see  that your mind loses the unpleasant energy that usually comes with feeling bored. It becomes more accepting of boredom. As you practise this, you will surely start feeling less bored on the whole. You might even begin to enjoy this me time!

You can also regularly do the practice of enjoying your life every day (page 21). This practice is another way to manage boredom even before it gets to you.

3

DEALING WITH ANXIETY

What Is Anxiety?

Anxiety is an umbrella term that people often use to speak about a wide range of emotions such as nervousness, uneasiness, worry, concern or stress. It is natural to feel such emotions when faced with challenging events or experiences over which we do not have much control. For example, it is natural to feel some anxiety during an exam.

When anxiety is present to a moderate degree, you are positively concerned about your revisions and giving your exams well. It can even motivate you to do well and study hard. However, when anxiety becomes overwhelming and is frequently experienced, it becomes a psychological condition that needs to be addressed so that you can function normally again.

For instance, if your anxiety is very high, you may feel so anxious before an exam that you may fall sick, become nauseous, or get panicky and fearful. It may become so overwhelming that you are not able to study well for the exam. If this is the case with you, talk to your parents and a doctor; there is lots of help available. You can also continue to do the practices shared in this book.

Anxiety is the response of our nervous system to a threat. When our nervous system feels we will be harmed somehow, it starts an internal reaction known as 'fight or flight'.

This means our body gets ready to either *fight* the threat or *run away* from the harmful situation. When this fight or flight reaction starts in our body, the heart starts to beat faster because it needs to pump more blood to get the body ready for the vigorous movements anticipated for combat or escape. Our legs get energized to run and move. Since we don't need the digestive function at that time, energy is taken away from it.

This fight or flight reaction is very beneficial when we are in the way of *actual harm*, because it helps us to deal with the threat. However, often due to our tendency to overthink, worry about the future and not stay present, our nervous system mistakenly thinks we might be in the way of harm. It thinks the imagined threat in our mental stories is real and activates the fight or flight reaction rather unnecessarily.

When this reaction starts up unwantedly and frequently, we become anxious. Anxiety can then become a habitual response of the nervous system, which means we can get accustomed to continuously being worried and anxious, as though something unpleasant is going to happen to us or some harm is going to befall us.

Through regular mindfulness practice, we can let the nervous system know that it does not need to be so anxious. When we breathe with full attention and stay present, we are not overthinking or worried. This informs the nervous system that we are in no danger, and it calls off the anxiety-creating fight or flight reaction.

With mindfulness meditation practice, your anxiety will surely decrease. The only condition is that you must practice regularly. Just doing the practices when you feel anxious will not help as much as regularly staying present, mindful and doing your daily meditation practices (pages 119–20).

In addition to your regular practice, you can apply the techniques given in this chapter when you are actively feeling anxious. Both will help you manage your anxiety better. You can use these exercises and practices even if you do not have much anxiety but still feel worried, tense or stressed.

EXERCISE: WHAT MAKES YOU ANXIOUS?

It is important to understand what situations or factors make you anxious. However, before you get into an exercise to understand that, please read Kritti's example below. This example will make the exercise that follows clearer.

Kritti is a sixteen-year-old girl in her first year of high school. She has been trained in Indian classical dancing for a few years. As a part of her training, she is expected to perform onstage. She is, however, very anxious and almost fearful of doing so. She thinks a great deal about what would happen if she does not perform well. What if she forgets a step or misses a beat? Her entire dance sequence will look terrible.

Her teacher will be so disappointed with her. The audience will feel they are wasting their time on a bad performance. Her co-dancers will evaluate each step and comment on her mistakes.

She has a mental image of standing on the stage looking blank and unable to dance. This makes her panic.

Now that you have read the above example to guide you, you can start the exercise:

Tick the boxes against the situations given below that make you anxious. These are just some examples. If what makes you anxious is not mentioned here, please write it in the space provided on the next page.

- ☐ Going to school
- ☐ Meeting new people
- ☐ Speaking or performing in front of a group of people
- ☐ Preparing or appearing for exams
- ☐ Waiting for results, like the final score of a game or a performance, or waiting for exam results
- ☐ Dealing with change, like changing houses, cities, schools; or starting a new class
- ☐ Having to manage stressful situations at home, like arguments among family members

Other situations that make you anxious:

_____

_____

Now try to describe your situation in a bit of detail. Doing this will help you clearly know why you feel anxious.

Just like Kritti has a mental image of going blank onstage and being unable to dance, examine your mental image about the situation that makes you anxious. If you do not have a mental picture, simply describe the situation. What is it that you fear? What is the worst that can happen?

Now that you have understood what makes you anxious, let us look at some essential points you need to remember while managing anxiety.

Three Points to Remember When Addressing Anxiety

Remembering these points will help you to maintain clarity when you are dealing with anxiety.

1. Do not try to avoid anxiety by avoiding the situation that makes you anxious

Referring to Kritti's example, if she avoids performing onstage so that she can feel less anxious, she will slowly lose all her confidence to do it.

Even if a situation is too overwhelming and you do end up avoiding it, try and calm yourself before facing it the next time. In the long run, *facing* your anxieties and fears will make you happy and confident.

If you persistently avoid situations that make you anxious, you will always fear the situation and lose your confidence.

For instance, if you are afraid of meeting new people, take time to practise mindfulness so that you become less anxious and are more prepared. Start by meeting smaller groups first. Take your time, but do not avoid meeting people altogether.

You can take small steps and be compassionate to yourself. But don't let your anxiety make decisions for you that are not good for you in the long run.

2. Do not distract yourself from feeling anxious

If you are feeling anxious, recognize it and go through the steps below to work with it. Don't try to push it away by playing games, watching TV, eating or doing something else. You can do all that later after you have spent at least some time understanding and staying with your anxiety.

3. Do not believe in all the negative thoughts when you are anxious

Remember, these are stories made up by the mind, and they are not true even if they may feel that way. For instance, Kritti forgetting her dance steps and people judging her are just imaginary stories and images resulting from her fears. They are not the truth.

What Should You Do When You Feel Anxious?

Do you know what is the biggest problem when we are dealing with an unpleasant emotion like anxiety? The idea that we should not have that emotion, that it is somehow wrong to feel anxious, or that fear or anxiety makes us weak.

This kind of thinking is a problem because it is completely untrue. If we start managing our fear or anxiety based on the idea that we should not have it in the first place, our methods to deal with it will not be helpful.

As a psychologist who has worked with adults and children for over twenty years now, I am telling you that anxiety and fear are a part of life. Just like so many other emotions. Some people are more anxious, others may tend towards sadness, and still others may feel more angry or jealous.

All emotions are just part of being human. They are also impermanent. They come and go. It is natural to feel any or all of them. When we work with our anxiety and fear with such openness, we start to feel better because our minds and bodies have stopped resisting the emotion. Instead, our energy is now invested in understanding it, rather than fighting it off.

If you understand this point well, you will do yourself a big favour. You will stop fighting anxiety. And in the method that follows, you will start to understand anxiety and make friends with it. Yes, all your feelings and emotions deserve friendship. Not a single one is excluded.

Our practice remains the same: Pause, Name, Accept and Support. So, when you feel anxious, go through the following steps:

1. **Pause**: Take a few deep breaths. Breathe into your belly. As you breathe in, let your belly fill up like a balloon. As you breathe out, let your belly deflate like a balloon. Do this for 7–10 breaths.

    When you breathe like this, you communicate to your nervous system that even though the situation provokes anxiety, it isn't potentially life-threatening like the nervous system is imagining to be. In turn, the nervous system will then start to help you by reducing the anxiety-creating fight and flight reaction.

2. **Name it:** Notice what you are feeling. Are you feeling anxious, or tense or afraid? Use the word that best describes your feeling. Now softly repeat this to yourself: 'I am scared.' Or 'I am anxious.'

   Acknowledging your feelings means telling your mind and body that you understand what is happening now. You are aware.

3. **Accept it:** Tell yourself that it is okay to feel anxious. You are definitely not alone. Many people feel anxious for so many different reasons. Sometimes even people who appear confident can feel quite anxious in certain situations.

4. **Support it:** Think of your anxiety as a little child inside you that is afraid. This child needs your support. Perhaps you can tell your anxiety: 'Don't worry, I will take care of you.' Or 'Don't worry, it's gonna be okay.'

   Maybe you can keep a hand on your chest and say 'It's okay' to the sense of anxiety or panic inside. Continue to take deep but slow and gentle breaths while supporting yourself.

   Take a moment to notice the sounds around you. Notice the things that you can see around you mindfully. Keep your feet flat on the ground. Doing this brings you into the present moment. It relaxes the nervous system and helps it realize that there is no threat in the *here and now*.

If you feel stiff and frozen because you are feeling fearful, then walk around very slowly, all the while noticing the connection of your feet with the ground. You can also move your arms slowly. This movement can help in moving the body out of a fearful space.

AN ADDITIONAL SUPPORT PRACTICE: VISUALIZATION OF THE LAKE

If you feel too anxious even to notice the ground or move, you can do this visualization exercise first. After this, you can go back to the four steps given above.

Read this contemplative poem to help you through this visualization practice.

THE LAKE

I see a lake,
Steady, calm and beautiful
Enriching the landscape.

The winds blow over it,
The rain disturbs its waters,
The birds and animals drink from it,
The children throw stones at it,
But everything is a mere ripple,
Momentary and short-lived.
Soon it returns to its true nature,
Still and peaceful.

I am like the lake.
All worries are merely ripples in me.
The winds of fear blow over me
for a while.
And then it is over.
I am calm, still and peaceful,
For that is my true nature.

Now imagine a calm, scenic lake. You are like this lake, peaceful and serene by nature. You may feel differently while you are anxious, but all fears and anxieties are just ripples on this lake.

Every time a thought that carries anxiety arises in you, notice a ripple on the lake. Let the ripple take its time. How long does it last? A short while? Maybe a little longer? No ripple can last forever. Ripples may happen again and again, but their nature is to come and go.

This is the nature of your anxiety. It comes and goes within you. But you are the lake; you are still, serene and so much more than your anxiety.

Like the lake knows ripples but is not the ripples, you are also the knower of your anxiety. You are the one who watches your anxiety arise, increase, reduce and leave. Like a witness. If you are the witness, how can you be the anxiety?

Remind yourself: I am the *knower* of anxiety; I am not the anxiety. I can watch the anxiety in my mind and body, but I don't have to own it. It is not me.

With practice, you will learn to stay with anxiety kindly and yet feel brave enough not to avoid the situations that create anxiety in you.

4

DEALING WITH JEALOUSY

What Is Jealousy?

Jealousy has both a thought and a feeling component.

- **Thought component**: You see a person and think that they are better than you in some way. Your mind tells you that they have something that you do not. Following this primary thought are thoughts about blaming yourself, judging yourself as inadequate or even criticizing the other person so that you feel better.
- **Feeling or emotion component**: When you feel jealous, you feel very unpleasant. Maybe a combination of sad, low, uneasy, angry and ashamed.

What are the kind of jealousy-filled thoughts one might have? Here are some examples:

- 'His football game is so much better than mine. When we play, everyone's eyes are only on him. I'm a pathetic player.'
- 'Oh, look at her dressed up to the gills! What a show-off!'
- 'There she goes, smooth-talking the teacher. No wonder Ma'am is so sweet to her!'

- 'Just because he is handsome and popular with the girls, he thinks no end of himself.'

Take a moment here to think of someone you feel jealous of. What are the thoughts in your mind about this person? Write them down here:

_____

_____

_____

_____

Now read on to understand your jealousy better.

Why Do We Get Jealous?

The human mind is conditioned to survive. Have you heard of the phrase 'survival of the fittest'? It means that only those who are 'fitter' than others will survive in the race for survival. We can interpret 'fitter' to mean 'better than others in many crucial ways'.

So our mind has learnt to watch everyone carefully and compare ourselves to others to see whether we are better than them or not. This is just how our brain has got wired. It has become a habit to compare, criticize and judge ourselves as inferior or superior.

While this strategy might have been beneficial earlier in the journey of evolution, it rarely serves the same function any more as most of us do not have to actively worry about physical survival! We have enough food, shelter and clothing, actually more than we need, and we have no wild animals to fear. We are more concerned now with thriving and being happy.

From a happiness point of view, this habit of watching others, comparing and criticizing is most unhelpful. As we have seen, nature has created all of us the way we are with our unique special qualities. Striving to be better than others instead of enjoying our gifts is a direct way to unhappiness. So, we have to remember this:

1. Our mind is simply speaking from its conditioning; we don't *have* to believe it.
2. Jealousy is only a voice in the head and a feeling in the body. There is no other reality to it. You can observe the voice in your head without believing in it. And you can support yourself through the unpleasant feeling in the body without making stories about it.

Working through Jealousy

1. Use your jealousy to understand more about yourself

When you feel jealous, do not simply believe the stories that get created in your mind about others. Instead, use jealousy as an opportunity to explore what is really happening with you.

Let's take an example of a jealousy-filled thought to understand this further. Let's say the thought in your mind is: 'His football game is so much better than mine. When we play, everyone's eyes are only on him.'

Now you have an opportunity to ask yourself, what about this person playing well is making you jealous? Are you wanting to play this sport well too? Or are you simply jealous of the attention this other player is getting? Questioning yourself in this way can help you a lot.

If it is really the game that you want to play well, then you can put your energy into actually doing better at it. At least you can try to improve your game to the best of your capacity. In that sense, you have used jealousy positively as a motivation to improve and excel.

If it is the adulation the other player is receiving that is making you jealous, you can remind yourself that this is just the competitive conditioning that all human beings have. This is not your fault. You can try to be kind to yourself and let it go. You can remind yourself, 'I am a masterpiece that nature created'—and that is the truth.

2.   Practice the method of dealing with difficult feelings

We have already gone through the pause, name, accept and support exercise several times so far. This exercise applies to all feelings. I have also explained how to apply it to different emotions (see chapter 1 and chapter 3 of this section).

This is a universal practice for all emotions, and therefore, you can apply it to jealousy too. Please do the practice right away if you are feeling jealous before reading further.

3.   Cultivate *mudita*—feeling joy in the joy of others

'Mudita' is a word in Sanskrit and Pali language that means 'feeling joy in the joy of others'. I am introducing it here for two reasons. The first reason is that it is a perfectly apt practice to help you through jealousy. The second reason is that you already have some experience in practising metta (page 89), which is feeling compassion for yourself and others. Metta practice is most helpful in laying a foundation for mudita. Metta itself is a very powerful tool for managing jealousy.

Moving on to mudita, we all believe that we are good people deep within and that we like others. But we quickly become jealous when someone else does well, especially if they do better than us. Do we ever stop to ask ourselves why others should not do better than us? Shouldn't others also get a chance to be happy? We are so involved in our own pleasure and pain that we forget others are just like us. They also want to do well and be happy. Mudita is a practice of understanding this and trying to feel joy for others when they are doing well.

Here is a practice that you can do when you are feeling jealous. It will help you to support yourself and develop mudita.

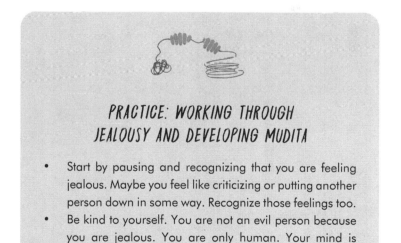

PRACTICE: WORKING THROUGH JEALOUSY AND DEVELOPING MUDITA

- Start by pausing and recognizing that you are feeling jealous. Maybe you feel like criticizing or putting another person down in some way. Recognize those feelings too.
- Be kind to yourself. You are not an evil person because you are jealous. You are only human. Your mind is

conditioned to feel jealous. Tell yourself that it is okay to feel this way. When you are jealous, you are also not feeling happy, and you need your own care and affection. Give this loving support to yourself.

- Support the feeling of jealousy through noticing and supporting your body sensations using movement and touch. You have learnt to do this well by now. Refer to the practice on working with difficult feelings (pages 143–44) if you need to review it.

  Stay with this practice until the jealousy reduces and you feel loved and understood by yourself. This is self-compassion, and it is an essential step before you can practise feeling happy for others. You have to learn to be gentle and kind to yourself, and only then can you be genuinely kind to others.

- Now that you feel a little better, think of how the person who has done better than you is feeling. Perhaps they got selected for an honour, did well at something or are being praised. They may be feeling happy right now.

  Remember that there are times when this other person also goes through jealousy, nervousness or the feeling of not being good enough. This is, however, their moment of some joy. Can you participate in it? Try to see if you can feel happy or at least a little glad for their happiness. Even if you cannot feel fully happy for them, try to mentally say, 'May you be happy and enjoy your moment.'

How we feel about other people is a reflection of how we feel within. When we feel happy for others, the open-hearted happy feeling becomes a part of us. When we feel jealous and competitive, our heart is closed and uneasy, and we are not satisfied with ourselves.

5

DEALING WITH BODY IMAGE DIFFICULTIES: LEARNING TO LOVE YOUR BODY

Some of us have a complicated relationship with our body. We like certain parts of our body, but not others. For instance, we may not like our weight or height. We may feel we are too fat or too thin, or too short or too tall. We may also not like a specific part of our body; perhaps we feel we have thin hair, a flat nose or skinny arms.

Not liking our body or parts of our body is what psychologists refer to as having body image difficulties.

In this chapter, let us learn to understand and helpfully relate to our bodies. But before we start, here is an example to make things clear. This time, it is a personal one, an example from my life.

MY ENCOUNTER WITH BODY IMAGE DIFFICULTIES

Let me tell you what I went through in school, concerning one aspect of my body. I always had thick, lovely hair as a child. Everyone I know used to admire my hair so much that I had come to believe that having thick hair was something to be very pleased or even proud about.

Then something weird happened. When I was in the fifth grade, I developed two bald patches on the scalp. It was a skin problem called alopecia. It wasn't anything serious, but it probably made me look quite strange. These bald patches were clearly visible through my hair.

In school, classmates would often come to me and ask me to show them the bald patches. It was a new thing for them. At home, my parents were very worried. They would regularly put medicines on the patches and try to get me to take responsibility for my medication. I wasn't too bothered and often would forget to apply medicine. When I forgot, they would get angry with me, telling me that I would continue to look weird if I didn't care for myself.

Then, after some months, the problem got worse. I lost an eyebrow. All the hair from one of my eyebrows suddenly disappeared. After some more months, I started losing the eyelashes on one side. Now I really started to look strange, with one eyebrow and one set of eyelashes missing. Everyone could see that something wasn't right with me.

No one really teased me in school, but I knew my classmates were finding my condition weird and sometimes talked about me to each other. When I went out for any social gathering, people would ask my mom what happened to me and look very sorry. 'A growing young girl and such an ugly looking condition,' they would say, with sympathy and pity. Everyone would suggest some kind of cure or treatment too.

I got injections on my eyebrows and went through continuous medication for years, but the condition did not resolve for at least four years.

On the surface, I neither showed concern nor seemed worried about the problem. It seemed like nothing was affecting me. But deep inside, I started to feel that I looked very weird and that I should hide myself, not participate in anything, not go anywhere and not expose myself to people, so they would not see my condition and ask questions about me.

Slowly, trying to hide became a way of life. At that time, I did not fully know that I was trying to hide; I came to this realization much later. I lived like that, with one eyebrow and a few bald patches, for four years, from fifth grade until ninth grade. Then, luckily, all my hair started growing back on its own.

This is an example of a body image difficulty. I was *ashamed* of looking a certain way.

Often, however, we don't even need to have a medical condition to be ashamed of ourselves or reject ourselves.

We may just not like some part or aspect of our body and feel that we are flawed.

My body is not great. I look weird or ugly. I look too thin or too fat or too dark. I hate this black mole on my cheek. My nose is too big. My eyes are too small.

These are all just judgements that our mind keeps habitually creating. Then we believe in these judgements and become depressed and unhappy.

Our mind is spinning stories about what's problematic with our body. It is only focusing on those aspects we do not like. But is that all there is to our body? What is the reality of our body?

A Realistic Picture of Our Body

Here is a realistic picture: our bodies are simply amazing! They help us move, eat, digest, breathe and enjoy life. Without the support of our bodies, we wouldn't be able to play, watch TV, read this book, talk to friends or do anything else. Our body is not an object to be gawked at and judged. Rather, it is the instrument through which we experience the world and express our uniqueness.

It is our mind's negativity bias (page 79) that makes us ignore all the beautiful things about our bodies and instead makes us focus on something that is not quite okay.

When we relate to our body in such a biased way, picking out its flaws, we are bound to feel down and sad.

Images in the Popular Media Make It Worse

On TV and in movies, we see many people who are very beautiful and have great bodies. We think this is how our faces and bodies should be and then become unhappy that we do not look as good.

Who are your role models on TV? Good-looking and fit people? Celebrities who have lovely hair and strong muscles? Do you want to be like them?

This is the 'ideal' body image always presented in the popular media and advertised in glossy magazines. We gradually start believing that this is how we need to be.

There is no problem in trying to have a healthy and fit body. One must have a good diet and exercise routine in order to take care of one's body. The problem lies in being *unhappy* with the body.

We have to understand that TV and movies do not depict reality. Actors on TV and in films put on a lot of make-up. The pictures are shot with all the proper lighting and are further edited to hide whatever 'flaws' can still be seen. The result is, we get 'flawless' and 'perfect-looking' people.

Actors often diet a lot, work out for hours a day and sometimes even take medication to remain slim. They even undergo surgeries to make certain parts of their bodies attractive. It isn't easy to look that way. A lot of pain is involved.

They do it because their job depends on it. Often, it is neither healthy nor natural for them to do this.

It is most definitely not realistic for us to try and follow in their footsteps. It makes no sense for us to only keep wanting an 'ideal' body and reject the wonderful and very useful body we already have.

If you had an Indie dog as a pet and someone else had a great-looking poodle, would you stop loving your dog because someone else's dog looks better? No, right? Your relationship with your pet is personal—your dog would love you, cheer you up, be your best buddy. So why do you stop loving your body because someone else's looks better? See, it makes no sense!

Let's do an exercise to understand how you relate to your body.

EXERCISE: DO YOU HAVE BODY IMAGE DIFFICULTIES?

Let's do a quick check. Tick the statements below that apply to you.

- [ ] I have felt that I look ugly on certain days.
- [ ] My friends dress up better and look cooler than me.
- [ ] I am weak and frail; I want to be muscular and strong.
- [ ] I am too short or too fat, or much darker than others.
- [ ] People are not noticing me because I don't look good.

☐ People are noticing my friend/sister/brother because they look better and smarter.

☐ My hair/nose/fingers/feet (or any other body part) are not of the right shape or size.

If you ticked any of the above statements, you believe your mind's stories about how your body is not good enough. You are unhappy with your body because of the exaggerated idea about how perfect your body should be.

Understand the Truth about Your Body

To change your relationship with your body, you have to first spend time understanding the truth about it.

When you feel critical about your body, you need to realize that these judgements are merely stories created by your mind and not the truth. These stories feel real because they have gathered power by being mentally repeated over the years, and now you firmly believe in them.

When you were born, you had no idea of how a body should be. You were quite happy with the way you were for many years as a child. What changed later?

As you were growing, certain aspects of your body were admired, and others were criticized. People said, 'Why is she putting on so much weight?' or 'Why is he still so puny?' or 'She has such lovely almond-shaped eyes.' You also heard other people being criticized or admired for their looks and physique. You perhaps saw your parents or other elders around you being very conscious of how they looked and appeared. You saw films and TV and saw how film stars were almost worshipped for their 'good looks' and bodies. You saw advertisements asking you to wear a particular kind of make-up or use a specific product to look good. Perhaps you even saw some people who were fair/tall or had 'good' bodies receive more attention from others.

Slowly, you started believing that you had to have an *ideal* body and look beautiful to be considered good. The result was that you began to scrutinize your own body and reject parts of it that you did not like. Perhaps, you even proudly started showing off aspects that you *did* like.

Unfortunately, you became yet another person in the world having an unhealthy relationship with the body, one more person trying hard to look perfect.

EXERCISE: LOOKING OBJECTIVELY

Carefully observe all the people around you. It doesn't matter if they are strangers or people you know. Look objectively at their bodies without judging them. What do you see? You will see that people have all kinds of bodies—fat, thin, round, square. They are of differing heights, have various shapes of necks, faces, noses, feet and all kinds of skin colours.

That is just how it is. It is quite silly even to think any one body is better than the other. No one person's body is ideal or perfect. We are all just as we are, as nature made us.

The only truth is that your body is your friend. It is always supporting you, and now it is time to realize how great your body is and return its support and friendship.

Develop a Healthy and Loving Relationship with Your Body

Here is a quick list of what you can do to start making friends with your body right away.

1. Take care of your body and stop rejecting it. It is truly your biggest support system.
2. Exercise well, not to look slim, but because you must help your body stay healthy, fit and energetic.
3. Eat things that nourish your body; eat vegetables and healthy food as a way of showing your body that you care for it.
4. Most importantly, remember that looking good is an inside job. The most beautiful people are internally peaceful. If you work on the inside correctly, the outside appearance will take care of itself. And working correctly on the inside means accepting and even cherishing what you have and what others have. Appreciate the things that nature has lovingly gifted to everyone. When you regularly do the meditation practices shared throughout the book, the part of being peaceful and accepting gets taken care of.

Work through Body Image Difficulties

If you have been judging yourself and rejecting some aspects of your body, now is the time to apologize to your body for treating it unfairly. Whenever you realize you are criticizing your body or feeling upset about looking a certain way, immediately tell your body, 'I am sorry I judged you. May you be well and happy.' Smile at the part of the body that you judged. Maybe you can even place your hand on it as a gesture of friendship and connection.

If you regularly feel upset about your body, here is a practice you can do to develop a loving and friendly relationship with it. It is a modified version of the body scan meditation practice (page 115). Instead of the body scan practice, do this practice for some time until you feel more positive about your body. You can then return to regularly practising the body scan as suggested earlier.

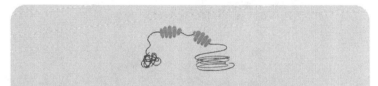

PRACTICE: SMILE AT THE BODY

This practice will help you create friendliness towards your body, and over time, you will develop more affection for your body.

You can ask a family member or a friend to read aloud the steps of the practice to you. Or record the steps in your voice and play it once you're ready to begin the practice. Alternatively, read it well to understand the practice and then attempt it on your own. Once you do this a few times, the practice will become familiar and easier.

1. Start by sitting on a chair or the ground comfortably, with your eyes closed.
2. Now, take a few deep breaths. Each time you breathe in, remember that this beautiful breath is helping you

to stay alive and well. Every time you breathe out, smile and relax your body a little. Do this for 5–10 breaths.

3. Now, move your attention to the area of your head, the entire area covered by your hair. Your brain is contained in the head region. It helps you walk, talk, see and eat. It is one of the most vital organs in your body, and it is working all the time. Smile at the head region and say, 'I thank you for taking care of me every day.' Now, stay connected, feeling the sensations in that area for a few seconds.

4. Now, focus your full attention on your face. Your face has most of your sense organs—eyes, ears, mouth and nose. These help you see, hear, taste and smell. They help you to go through your day smoothly. Smile at your face lovingly and say, 'I thank you for taking care of me every day.' Now, stay connected, feeling the sensations in your face for a few seconds.

5. Now, move your attention to your arms. Your arms help you eat, brush, play, paint, dance and perform so many other activities. Life would be so difficult if you wouldn't have arms. You cannot take them for granted. Take a moment to think of all the things your arms help you with and, with gratitude, smile at them and say, 'I thank you for taking care of me every day.' Now, stay connected, feeling the sensations in your arms for a few seconds.

6. Now, shift your attention to your whole front torso, from your neck to your chest and belly. Many of your organs

are here. Every day, these organs are hard at work so that you have the energy to study and play and enjoy life. So, thank all these organs. Smile at them and say, 'I thank you for taking care of me every day.' Now, stay connected, feeling the sensations in your torso for a few seconds.

7. Next, turn your attention to the back of your body, from the upper back down to the lower back. Your back contains your spine. You would collapse in a heap without your spine. It supports your whole body, keeping it erect when needed and allowing it to bend when needed. Smile and say to your back, 'I thank you for taking care of me every day.' Now, stay connected, feeling the sensations in your back for a few seconds.

8. You can now focus on the seat of the body and your legs. The seat of the body contains parts of the body associated with excretion. All the toxins that are not good for you and the waste materials are removed from your body, leaving you healthy and ready to receive new food. You can enjoy your food only if these areas of your body work tirelessly.

   Also, your legs give you constant support; they help you walk, run and play. Visualize all the good things your lower body does for you and say, 'I thank you for taking care of me every day.' Smile at it and stay feeling connected to it for a few seconds.

9. You have now finished appreciating and thanking your entire body. Now take your attention to that one aspect of your body that disturbs you the most. It could be your

weight, height, your hair, nose or skin colour. Focus your full attention on that one aspect.

Remind yourself again how your body works tirelessly to keep you well and functional. Is it not unfair to be upset about something so minor? Smile at that aspect of your body and say, 'I am sorry, I have not loved you enough. I am sorry I have been unkind to you by disliking you. I will try to remember how kind my body is to me.' Now smile at that part and stay connected to it, watching the sensations for a few seconds.

10. End your practice by taking a few deep breaths, smiling and relaxing every time you breathe out.

This is a beautiful practice to help you become kind towards your body. When you focus on remembering the wonderful ways in which your body supports you every day, even without you caring much for it, you will gradually start to love your body. Your body will also respond by healing and becoming healthier.

Body Shaming

While we are learning how to show love and respect to our bodies, it is important to speak about body shaming.

Body shaming is the act of teasing, mocking or criticizing someone because of how they look. When you tease someone calling them names like 'fatso' or 'shortie', even in jest, it is considered body shaming.

When you pass comments like, 'His nose is so big' or 'Her breasts are so flat', you are body shaming people.

No one likes being judged and teased about their body. Not you and not anyone else.

Sometimes, when we tease people, we may not intend to hurt them. We may not even remember it the next moment. But guess who does not forget? The person who is being body shamed. In fact, sometimes a single incident like this can scar someone for years to come.

Just as we are sensitive to being teased about our bodies, we also need to be sensitive to others and consciously remember not to body shame them.

As discussed at length in Part I, this will naturally happen if we remind ourselves that all bodies are precious and created by nature, exactly as they were intended. And this applies to you and everyone else. This is why this book is titled *You Are Simply Perfect!*

6

UNDERSTANDING AND WORKING THROUGH ADDICTION

What Is Addiction?

Simply speaking, addiction is a habit that people are unable to control after a while, even if it starts to have many negative results or consequences.

When we speak of addiction to harmful things, we usually think only of cigarette or alcohol addiction and people who cannot control these bad habits. While these are certainly addictions, there can be many more kinds of addictions. One of the most common ones at your age is internet addiction, which can include watching TV shows and movies, being on social media, or playing games for too long and not being able to stop even when you need to.

Another common addiction is food addiction, which is not about eating when you are hungry but when you just can't refrain from responding to your cravings.

There are many other damaging addictions too, which are not uncommon at your age.

Why Do You Need to Know about Addiction?

Firstly, you need to know about addiction so that you can recognize if you are already addicted to something and address it right away.

Learning about addiction will also help you to recognize when some habit starts to get addictive for you. When you recognize an addictive tendency early, you can work to prevent it from growing and taking over your life.

Finally, knowing about addiction can also help you to understand addiction in others and relate to them in a helpful way.

How Does Addiction Begin?

Addiction begins slowly and insidiously. Insidiously means very quietly, without anyone recognizing it, but with a lot of potentially harmful effects.

Let us take an example to understand how addiction can start.

Shaila was a quiet child in eighth grade who felt that she did not fit in with her classmates at all. She hardly had any friends in school. She just knew a few classmates with whom she would spend time so she wouldn't feel completely alone.

At some point, she started using an online chatting app and found that she enjoyed chatting with strangers.

She found that in a virtual world, she could find acceptance more easily, especially when chatting with boys much older than her.

Initially, it was just one person. Then, slowly, she was simultaneously chatting with many. She was giving out some confidential personal details to these people. She was finding ways to contact them even outside the online chatting portals.

Gradually, she started to become addicted to chatting. She could not focus on anything else except getting online. Each day, she would wait for school to end, to come back home and chat. Then, the COVID pandemic of 2020 happened, and all over the world, there were lockdowns. This meant more time at home, more computer time and more chatting time.

She gradually lost interest in studying. Over time, she stopped doing her homework too. She would only wait for messages from the people she was chatting with.

Even after the lockdown eased, she did not want to go outside and interact with others from her neighbourhood. The people she hung out with in her building were not as much fun as these people who made her feel important and special.

As she met new people, she started to get even more careless with her personal details. She started sharing more and more information with these strangers. She also started sharing her pictures. She soon became obsessed with clicking selfies to be able to share them with her online friends.

She also started to get quite restless. If one person wasn't online, she would try to contact another. If she couldn't find someone she wanted to chat with online, or if they did not respond to her pictures or messages, she would get very angry with them. She would send them spiteful messages. She would be snappy at home and feel very miserable. She would only feel better when someone admired her pictures or sent a message that made her feel important.

She wanted more and more of the attention she was getting virtually and very little of the real world she was actually living in. She no longer wanted to visit her relatives, play with her cousins or go out for dinner with her parents. She started to make excuses, saying she had homework to do or was not well so that she could stay at home and chat.

This is how addiction classically works. It starts slowly, as a pleasurable activity. However, if we do not recognize it and take action to stop it, it has the power to take over our life.

Shaila may think, 'What is the problem if the addiction is keeping me happy?' But is that true? Is this really happiness?

We know the answer to this since we have clearly understood the difference between pleasure and happiness in Part I (page 23). You can read it again so that it can help you decide whether Shaila is choosing happiness or pleasure.

This is not happiness; it is an addiction to pleasure that creates deep unhappiness in the long run. We can clearly see this in Shaila's case. Initially, Shaila was liking the attention of others. But she gradually became so dependent on that attention that she was miserable when she did not get it. She became restless, stopped living her life and interacting with real people. Instead, she became obsessed with just getting attention from strangers online.

This is what addiction does to us. Our growth in life stops. Instead of learning new ways of enjoying life and living in a balanced way, we become pleasure seekers. We get hooked on that one source of pleasure that is now slowly becoming harmful for us. It is taking us away from a good life, from making new friends, from learning new skills.

It is the same with people who are addicted to any drug or substance. Initially, there is pleasure—a nice, heady and relaxed feeling. Slowly, the person's brain becomes used to feeling good only when it gets that drug or substance. Without the substance, the mind gets agitated and starts to crave it.

Slowly, life becomes about that substance. Life becomes about seeking that high, and real, everyday life does not seem interesting any more. If you speak with people who are addicted to drugs, they will tell you that they have stolen, lied and cheated to get money for drugs so that they can feel the pleasure. These poor choices are all made because people get so hooked to the substance that they cannot live without it. This is addiction at its very extreme.

But addiction does not start with such a dark picture. It starts lightly in a seemingly harmless way. There is an indulgence one or two times, which begins so slowly that you feel you are in complete control when actually, you are slowly handing over control to your addiction.

Shaila is also moving towards this extreme. She is already lying and hiding things to get pleasure. She needs to realize this before it is too late.

Why Do People Get Addicted?

The reason a person gets addicted is that getting pleasure is *easy*. Everything else needs time and effort, but the substance or behaviour we are addicted to gives us immediate pleasure without any effort. We become used to getting pleasure without effort.

If you need to learn a skill or make friends or eat healthy, you need to put in some effort. A lot of things that are good for you need some effort. Even taking a few deep breaths and meditating needs a relaxed kind of effort.

But watching TV, for example, is instant pleasure. Just sit and switch it on and the pleasure starts. So, it is easy to become addicted to TV.

We leave behind things that require effort. We stop being creative or trying out difficult but meaningful things. The pleasurable activity keeps tempting us, and we keep giving in to the temptation until we become too dependent on it.

Once we are *dependent* on something, our brain gets wired to keep going to it for more pleasure. The more we give in to that temptation, the more addicted we become. It is a downward spiral.

How Can You Know Whether You Are Addicted?

The first step in dealing with addiction is to recognize whether you are addicted. Even if you are not fully addicted, do you have any addictive tendencies you need to be careful about?

How can you know that? Here are a few pointers; check whether these are applicable to you:

1. Is any one activity or substance starting to feel like it is the most enjoyable thing in life, like being on the internet, watching TV, eating desserts or some substance that your friends introduced you to?
2. Do other daily life activities feel uninteresting in comparison to that one thing/activity/substance?
3. Do you spend a lot of time thinking about when you can do that activity or get that substance again? For example, if you are addicted to food, you will spend a lot of time thinking about when you would get a break and when you would get to eat. Or if you are addicted to TV, even while you are playing outside or doing some work, you will keep thinking about when you will get to watch TV.

4. Do you hide from your parents and try to do that activity or use that substance?
5. Do you know that you are overdoing something, like watching too much TV or overeating but cannot give it up? Maybe you are eating even when you are not hungry. Or playing a virtual game for too long, even though it is no longer as exciting.
6. Do you know intuitively that what you are doing is not correct? Maybe you even feel guilty or embarrassed about doing it, but you just cannot stop.

If your answer to some of the above questions is yes, you may be dealing with some addictive tendency or even a full-blown addiction.

The positive side of realizing this is that your effort can bring you out of this. You are not 'bad' because you are stuck in a habit. People who are addicted are not bad people; they are simply stuck in a pleasure-seeking loop or habit that is now becoming harmful for them.

What Can You Do to Help Yourself?

Throughout the book, we have addressed situations by understanding them correctly and then doing a helpful practice. Let's bring the same two aspects to dealing with addiction: right understanding and right practice.

Right understanding

This is about understanding your addiction. When you correctly understand your addiction, you can deal with it better. Addiction is all about urges and impulses. An urge or impulse is that deep inner need that makes you want something immediately.

In the case of Shaila, the urge is to chat. If you are addicted to TV, the urge is to watch TV, and you need to do it as soon as possible.

This is how an urge may express itself: you may be studying, you get the sudden desire to play a game on your phone or open a social media app.

This is an urge. It comes up suddenly, and it is related to the pleasure you are hooked on to. The urge is to get yourself that pleasure immediately.

But urges, especially repetitive urges, can come from deep emotions. For instance, Shaila feels *out of place* in real life. She feels like she does not belong and her presence does not matter to anyone. While chatting, she gets the appreciation and attention she craves. So, her urge to chat with strangers comes from her deep need for attention, belonging and perhaps even love.

If she felt happier in her life, she would not want to escape it to seek pleasure from chatting with strangers.

Another example is eating food when we are not hungry. Often, we snack not because we are hungry but because we are bored or feeling low. You feel bored, so you pick up a packet of chips. The urge to eat the chips comes from wanting to escape boredom or the low feeling. When you eat because you are bored and not because you are hungry, your body does not actually need that food, and you cause disturbance to your body. If you repetitively follow this urge, you may develop food addiction, where food is used to perpetually push away uncomfortable feelings.

Similarly, in many examples of addiction, you will find that urges arise because you don't want to *feel* difficult emotions, and instead, you want to feel pleasure.

People who are addicted to selfies desire to overshare and post a new picture multiple times a day when they feel restless or stressed. It is a way of escaping stress. Or they do so to appear and look very cool and hip. But if someone is obsessively taking selfies to appear cool and prove a point, it means they are not feeling very cool about who they are. They are actually trying to escape feeling inadequate.

If we have to overcome our addiction, we have to learn to relate to our life and our emotions. We cannot escape our life and get hooked on pleasure. We need to remember that while pleasure may feel good in the short term, this addiction will make our lives quite painful in the long run.

So, here's what we do. After we have the right understanding, we take the right action.

Right action

Getting out of addiction can be similar to getting out of a deep ditch that you have fallen in. If you accidentally fall into a ditch, you wouldn't resign to being there. You'd try every method of getting out, wouldn't you?

Similarly, when you are addicted, you mustn't resign and accept your addiction. You commit to getting out and try every method possible.

Getting back to the analogy of the ditch, what would you need to do to get out of a deep ditch?

Broadly speaking, you would do two things:

1. **Ask for help:** You would need to call out for help so that someone can support you. Maybe they could drop you one end of a rope.
2. **Help yourself:** You would need to help yourself by putting in the effort to climb out using the rope.

Similarly, when dealing with addiction, you go through precisely these two steps:

1. Ask for help

Talk to your parents or an elder in your family whom you trust. You could even ask a friend's parent if you trust them. Any adult who can understand you would do.

I understand your worry that your parents may get angry with you and judge you. They may even feel disappointed in you and lose trust in you. And yet, as a psychologist who has worked with several individuals who have been battling addiction, I can tell you this: no matter how bad it feels to lose face in front of others, it is still infinitely better than staying addicted and losing your entire life to addiction. That's what addiction does. It ruins your life!

Ask your parents to take you to a psychologist who will definitely be more understanding. A psychologist is professionally trained to help you overcome addiction.

Telling people about your addiction is a step that needs a lot of courage, but changing any unhelpful pattern and creating a good life for yourself always requires courage. Once other people are involved, your addiction is no longer a private thing, which is great, because then you will surely get the help you need to get over it.

If you are reading this book, trying to find a way to be your own friend and deal with your addiction, you are already quite brave. Only courageous people try to look within and create inner change. Don't let your mind or anyone else tell you otherwise.

2. Help yourself

Your willingness to recognize and get out of your addiction is half the battle already won. Now you need to use your own mind and body to put in the right effort to deal with your addiction. In this book, so far, we have already looked at many ways of being calm, focused and staying in the present. All of them are very helpful in overcoming addictive behaviour.

When you are mindful, you are connected to the details of your everyday life. You are able to enjoy small things in your day-to-day life. Your life becomes more peaceful and happy. You don't need to seek pleasure to escape your life. Gradually, as your brain tunes in to this way of being, your addictive tendencies naturally reduce.

Urge surfing is an important practice that can help you with addiction. It is a way to stay with your urges without giving in to them. However, this needs you to have done your body scan practice and breathing meditation practice regularly.

Since urges are sensations in the body, staying with them requires an ability to notice and stay with unpleasant body sensations. If you have done the body scan practice (page 115) previously, you have practised staying with your body sensations.

Urge surfing

Before you get into the practice of urge surfing, ask yourself this: how do you experience an urge? Let's say you are studying, but suddenly, you feel like browsing videos online. What happened here was that an urge arose in you to move away from studying and towards watching videos. But how did you experience this urge?

On introspecting, you will realize you do not pay any attention to the urge at all. Instead, you quickly invest all your energy in either satisfying that urge or sometimes even resisting it. For example, when you get an urge to browse videos while studying, you just stop your studies and quickly move to your phone or tablet to browse videos. Or you just power through your studies, trying to resist the urge. In both cases, you do not notice the urge; you do not know its experience.

Urge surfing means neither giving in to the urge nor resisting it. It is about being aware and mindful of it. It is about staying with the urge.

To do this, you need to pay attention to what really happens after the urge to browse videos arises and before you move to pick up the phone to satisfy that urge. What happens in that gap?

That gap is of monumental importance as both the possibility of addiction and freedom from addiction lie in that gap. Normally, this gap is difficult to recognize and very easy to miss. However, when you practise mindfulness, with some effort, you can learn to recognize it.

So let us further examine what happens in this gap, using the same example. You are sitting with your textbooks and an urge comes up in you; you want to browse videos. This is where you need to pause. Become aware that this urge to move away from studies and towards the videos is present now.

What is the experience of this urge? There is probably some boredom with what you are doing, some restless energy in your body that is pushing you to move your attention and reach out to a phone or tablet.

This is where, instead of moving to satisfy the urge, you can stay while observing your urge with awareness and curiosity. You can ask yourself, 'What is happening in my body right now?'

Feel the body sensations that are pushing you to pick up your phone. Simply accept that you feel restless and want to move, but you are going to wait and watch the restlessness for some time, at least. You are not going to give in to it.

You can watch the restlessness by focusing on your breath. Maybe you can take deep breaths filling up your belly.

When practising like this, you have certainly stopped studying, but you haven't given in to the urge to browse videos.

As you practise, this is what is likely to happen: you will realize that you have a strong urge to move. But as you pay attention to your breath, breathe into your belly and notice your body sensations; it will cause the urge to gradually lose its power. It will still be there, but it will lose its strength. Just as a wave settles down after the first roar and slowly becomes very quiet, this impulse will do the same.

It may come again after a few minutes, like another wave. Your practice remains the same. Pause. Breathe. Notice the body sensations that come up. Stay.

Urge surfing is all about practising again and again.

Developing this capacity to stay with your urges, knowing them, supporting them but not giving in to them, will help you win your battle with addiction.

Learning to surf your urges is much like learning to surf waves. People who learn surfing have to be ready to fall several times before they learn to smoothly ride a wave. Much practice is needed with the understanding that it will take time.

It is the same with urge surfing. It will take practice and patience to get the hang of it, to succeed in completely staying aware of your urges and not giving in to them. In the process, you may give in to your urge several times and feel guilty. Instead of guilt, which really doesn't help, simply make a resolve to try surfing your urge again the next time it arises. Repeated attempts and practice will surely help you overcome your addiction.

Kabir encourages us not to be at the mercy of our mind's stories and urges. He says:

Man ke mate mat chaliye,
Man ke mate hain anek.
Jo man par sawaar rahe,
So sadhu koi ek.

This means:

Don't let the mind overpower you, pay no attention to its urges and impulses; it has too many urges.

It is a rare person, a real strong character, who develops the capacity to ride the mind to control it.

This is the kind of strong character you will develop if you patiently and persistently surf the urges of addiction, without giving in to them.

You have so far learnt how to work through addiction with the right understanding and the right practice. Here are some points that will further assist you in your efforts:

1. **Meditate regularly**: Changing addictive tendencies needs more than momentary practice. Simply practising urge surfing when an urge comes up will not be enough. You have to combine this with a mindful life in general and regular meditation practice (page 67). Only with an entire perspective change will real shifts take place in life. Not only will your addiction reduce but also your overall sense of joy and well-being will increase.

2. **Practise metta**: Practising kindness (page 91) towards yourself is very helpful for dealing with addiction. As you read earlier, people often get addicted when there is some deep emotional pain they are trying to escape. Also, when you are addicted, you don't feel very good about yourself. You may feel guilty. This is the time that you need to be your own best friend. Only love and compassion will help in healing the pain that is underlying your addiction. Don't blame yourself or criticize yourself for having an addiction. That is creating a harsher inner environment that will worsen the pain. Instead, diligently work towards overcoming your addiction, all the while wishing well for yourself.

3. **Try to spend time doing other activities you find enjoyable:** Take a course, join a class, spend time with friends or relatives and try to enjoy day-to-day activities by being mindful. Addiction isolates you, separates you from engaging with life. You stop living and only think about the next high. Re-engaging with life will help you reclaim the joy that is always present in the regular daily activities.

4. **Remember that there is no quick fix:** Even if you put in all effort, your addiction will not disappear overnight. Your brain is involved. It is hooked to pleasure. It will keep craving it. You may feel you are trying so hard and still ending up succumbing to your addiction. Don't lose heart. Try to keep at it and take small steps. For instance, if you are addicted to carbonated soft drinks, reduce the consumption. If you tend to binge on junk food, mindfully eat it a bit less. As you reduce it slowly, it will stop continuing to be an addiction.

5. **Finally, remind yourself that you are nature's child:** You are wonderful, lovely and special. Even if you are addicted to something, this truth does not change. Nature cares for you. Care for it back by working on your addictions and keeping yourself healthy. If you really want to get over your addiction, nature will provide help in different ways. Perhaps the fact that you are reading this chapter is in itself nature's way of helping you.

7

UNDERSTANDING BULLYING AND DEALING WITH IT

What Is Bullying?

Bullying means trying to physically or psychologically harm someone by dominating, teasing, forcing, threatening or blackmailing them. Bullying is often repetitive. It is done by people who see themselves in a position of some power and is directed towards those who seem less powerful.

If you are regularly teased, spoken to rudely, made fun of, or put down often by a person or a group of people, then you are probably being bullied.

The person bullying you could be a part of your family, school, classes or associated with you in some other way.

Here is an example for you to understand bullying better:

Thirteen-year-old Pranay was very fond of playing football and was often found practising on the football ground. His coach assigned him to a team that included Sanjay. Sanjay was a popular boy with a mean streak. He was the self-appointed leader of a gang of boys who would pick on others in the school, and have a laugh at their expense. Sanjay found Pranay to be timid and an easy target. He started picking on Pranay and teasing him. Sometimes, he would even throw the ball at him in a way that hurt him. In other instances, Sanjay would intentionally give him a hard push while playing and make it seem accidental. Sanjay's friends merely laughed and enjoyed the spectacle.

Pranay complained to the coach. The coach, however, had not seen Sanjay actively bullying Pranay and took it lightly. Pranay was feeling hurt and gradually getting demotivated to play.

Also, after Pranay complained to the coach, Sanjay and his group of friends started teasing him even more. They mocked him by saying, 'Baby, go to your papa and complain.'

Eventually, the situation became unbearable for Pranay and he started making excuses to not play football.

When we come across such examples, we are clear who is right and who is wrong. Who is the victim and who is the mean bully. However, just knowing that, and being angry with the bully helps no one.

We need to understand bullying in a deeper and slightly different light.

As always, we will try and get a perspective on what is really going on. We will try to understand why people bully others, so we have some insight into the mind of the bully. We will discuss what you can do if you are being bullied. We will also learn to recognize whether you are bullying others, knowingly or unknowingly, and explore what you can do about it.

Let's get started.

Why Do People Bully Others?

When you are being bullied, you feel so very helpless. You may also feel angry and frustrated. The person bullying you may seem stronger, more powerful and in control.

But now, I will let you in on a secret that psychologists have known for a while. Bullies are most certainly unhappy people. Imagine how unhappy a person must be if their way of having fun is by making another person unhappy. That is what bullies are doing, aren't they? They are making themselves feel better by making someone else miserable. They are finding a way to vent their own frustrations.

In our example, if Sanjay were peaceful and happy with himself, he would not choose to trouble Pranay. There would be no reason to. Instead, Sanjay is probably frustrated and unhappy on the inside and tries to feel strong and powerful by making Pranay feel small and powerless.

Sanjay's friends who are participating in the bullying are very weak, if not deeply unhappy themselves. They are trying to belong together, make Sanjay feel good by encouraging him, in order to be a part of the gang. They don't have the strength to question what is right or to go against Sanjay. They are weak because they need to have fun at someone else's expense. If even one boy from this group of people was a strong person, who was peaceful and happy within himself, he would refuse to participate. Maybe he would even be brave enough to object.

People who are peaceful do not harm others. This is a simple truth. Apply this to yourself: When you are in a bad mood because let's say you had an argument with your parents, what kinds of things do you do? You get irritated and you may push the door hard, kick the stones on the road or snap at others who try to speak with you. Do you do that when you have just had your favourite dessert? Of course not!

You see, how you feel is reflected in your behaviour clearly. When you are unhappy, your behaviour becomes destructive and harmful to yourself and to others. When you are joyful and happy, your behaviour automatically becomes less harmful, and very often, also helpful.

It is the same with bullies. Their harmful behaviour is a reflection of their inability to deal with their own unhappiness. Perhaps they have some difficulty in life that we do not know about. Perhaps they have learnt that being aggressive is the only way to hide their weakness. Perhaps they feel unloved and rejected by someone. There could be so many reasons that we may never learn about and sometimes, even those who bully others may not realize what makes them behave like that.

Research has shown that there is a lot of trauma in the history of prison inmates. This means that they have been through very painful life events. Such research shows that people who have committed criminal offences, which include harming and injuring others seriously, or even killing others, have been in a lot of pain themselves.

All this points to the conclusion that happy people do not harm or bully others and do not derive any positive feelings from the misery of others.

This perspective helps our mind to stop creating false stories about ourselves and the people who bully us. We stop believing that we are less powerful or that they are more powerful. We don't judge ourselves as weak and them as strong. We recognize they are hurting us because of their own unhappiness. Their behaviour is not about us at all, it is about them.

Even if we still have to confront the painful situation of being bullied, this kind of realistic understanding of the situation, makes us feel a bit stronger.

How Can You Deal with Bullying?

When it comes to bullying, the right course of action can be divided into two aspects:

- Enlisting the support of adults
- Handling the bullying yourself

Let us understand both aspects.

Enlisting the support of adults

When the bullying is severe and involves physical harm, threat or blackmail, you absolutely must enlist the support of adults. There are a lot of pointers on the internet to help you with this. Here are some basic ones:

1. **Confide in an adult:** Tell your parents or an adult you trust about the bullying. If it involves mocking and teasing, maybe the adults in your life won't be able to help much, but it is always good to keep them informed. If the bullying is severe, where someone is harming you or threatening you, they will definitely be able to step in and help you quickly.

   Don't worry about appearing weak if you take help from adults. You are not weak. Bullying is genuinely a very difficult situation to deal with and you need all the support you can get.

2. **Tell more than one adult:** Don't get disheartened if you tell one adult and they take you lightly. Tell a teacher, your parents, a relative, an elder cousin, a friend's parent you are close to or any adult you trust. Tell more people so

that someone might take notice. For instance, in Pranay's situation, he only complained to the coach. The bullying he was facing was painful and was actually also involving some physical harm. Pranay would have had better chances of getting help if he had told several adults. At least somebody would have understood the seriousness of the situation.

3. **Don't be afraid that the adults will judge you**: This point is particularly applicable if bullying is in the form of blackmail. If you are being blackmailed for something you did, you could be afraid of telling your parents about it. You may feel concerned that if you tell them about the bullying, they will also learn of your actions that were not appropriate. Here again, remember, it is always better to put the truth out there and be free rather than hide the truth and become a target for blackmail.

Your parents may judge you. You may also have to face a lot of unpleasantness at home, but overall they are able to accept you more than you give them credit for. They have been your age and have gone through similar situations.

Handling the bullying yourself

When the bullying involves verbal mocking and teasing, often adults don't take it seriously or believe kids will learn to sort it out on their own.

Undoubtedly, this is not easy for you, as even teasing and mocking can cause psychological harm. But here is where you will receive less support and will need to build your own resilience and defence against the person bullying you. The entire purpose of this section is to provide you with tools to build inner resources that can help you deal with bullying.

Let us use an example to guide us through this process:

Sarah and Aditi were friends in the ninth grade. Sarah really enjoyed Aditi's company. Aditi was cool and hung around with other really cool people. In Aditi's company, Sarah got to hang out with other cool friends too. Aditi also dressed in a trendy way and Sarah admired her sense of dressing. When hanging out with Aditi, Sarah would put a lot of effort into dressing up well and looking good.

Aditi told Sarah all about her latest crush, the problems at home and other personal stuff. Sarah liked being Aditi's special person and confidante. It made her feel special because Aditi did not confide in anyone else.

However, at times, Sarah felt hurt at the way Aditi treated her, especially when others were around. When Sarah and Aditi were alone, Aditi was really friendly to Sarah, but when they were hanging out in a group, Aditi picked on Sarah or put her down by making jokes at her expense. She found reasons to criticize Sarah, dismiss her ideas, make sarcastic remarks about her sense of dressing or her appearance, or just laugh at her behaviour.

At first, Sarah tried to laugh at herself, made light of it and ignored it. However, this was becoming a regular occurrence. Sarah was confused. Did Aditi like her or didn't she? Why would she put her down in front of others, especially when Sarah was her only confidante, a keeper of her secrets?

Slowly, Sarah's confusion turned into deep hurt as Aditi continued to ridicule her in front of others.

We are seeing this situation from Sarah's eyes, so we cannot possibly imagine why Aditi is behaving the way she is.

However, we know that Sarah is feeling hurt. Her best friend is bullying her, but the bullying is not clear. Sarah is receiving mixed signals. Sometimes, she is made to feel special and at other times, she is teased and made to feel small.

This is not an uncommon situation. The person who is bullying us may sometimes also be a friend or even a family member with whom we have some good times as well.

If you are reading this chapter because you are being bullied, go through the reflection exercises throughout this section. This will help you get more clarity. Reflection spaces are provided at several points for you to examine your personal situation and write about it.

Are you going through any situation where you are being bullied? Write it down here:

_____

_____

_____

_____

Now let us examine the various ways in which we can handle bullying. All the while, we will use Aditi and Sarah's example to keep it practical and easy to understand. Also, you will have space to reflect on how you can apply the knowledge to your situation.

1. Do not pretend that you are not being bullied

Sometimes we believe that it is safer to continue being bullied than to confront the situation. It requires a lot of courage to complain to an adult, to confront the bully and to deal with all the difficult consequences of such confrontation. So we pretend that nothing untoward is happening, it is all okay and we quietly let the bullying continue. This is the most unwise choice.

When you pretend that all is well, you are non-verbally communicating to the person bullying you that you are *okay* to be treated in this way. This is not what you want to communicate. Instead what you want to let them know is whether or not they respect you, you do respect yourself.

In Sarah's case, pretending that Aditi's behaviour is not a problem and sticking around with her as a friend would be the most unwise choice. If she chose this, she would be exposing herself to more bullying, keep tolerating it and over time become very angry and bitter.

Also, not confronting Aditi would mean she is okay to be put down in front of others and laughed at. This wouldn't be a loving and respectful way for Sarah to treat herself.

Reflection Space

Reflect for a while on this point. Are you in a situation where you allow someone to bully you and still stay friends with them, and where you don't stand up for yourself?

Take a moment to contemplate and write about it here:

_____

_____

_____

_____

2. Don't blame yourself for being bullied

Do not ever believe what the bully says about you. Don't doubt your own worth. People who bully others have learnt the art of making people feel terrible about themselves. Their purpose is to feel superior by making others feel inferior and inadequate.

Don't buy into that false narrative or story. A bully's mind is also just like anyone else's, full of untrue, judgemental, cooked-up stories. When they put you down, they are exhibiting the problematic tendencies of their own mind. You have worked so very wisely with your mind. If you have been practising so far with the book, you already exercise caution in believing your own mind's stories. Why would you then give so much importance to the false stories of another person's mind?

In Sarah's case, since she receives mixed signals from Aditi, she could get into self-doubt. She may think, 'Aditi usually likes me, maybe she is making negative remarks about my clothes or my appearance because I really don't look good or don't dress well. Maybe I really have those flaws.' This could again lead to accepting Aditi's bullying. Here, Sarah needs to remember that she is beautiful and special exactly as she is. Aditi's judgements are Aditi's problem. They just don't matter!

Reflection Space

Do you believe in what the person who bullies you says about you? Do you end up doubting yourself, believing you are inadequate, weak, powerless or not good enough in some way? Write down your thoughts here:

_____

_____

_____

_____

3. Set clear boundaries

Once you have decided not to accept the bullying and realized you are not to be blamed, the next step is to set some boundaries. What does setting boundaries mean? This means that you will need to understand what you can tolerate and what is too much for you to bear and then take some action. You will need to find ways of showing the person who is bullying you that you will not tolerate their behaviour.

Now it all starts to get tough. This is no easy task, and yet, you cannot simply keep allowing this person to bully you. You have to do something. At least try something.

Often, fighting back with a bully, saying negative things to them or showing anger may not work. A person who bullies others derives satisfaction from their misery. If you show that you are angry and are getting triggered by their words, it can sometimes end up giving the bully more impetus to trouble you.

You can try to calmly verbally communicate that you are not willing to accept such behaviour from them.

This calmness will come easier if you have been practising meditation for a while. This method may or may not work, but it is certainly worth an attempt.

Calm communication sometimes works, especially if the person bullying you is not too serious about it, does not intend to really hurt you, is doing so in jest or values your friendship.

If the person's intention in bullying you is to make you feel terrible, then calmly speaking won't work. In such a case, silence and complete ignorance can be powerful tools. Completely stop engaging with the person or group of people who are bullying you. They can say what they want. They just don't matter and nothing they say is to be believed.

This power of not relating to someone is always with *you*. No one can force you to relate and engage with anyone. Their behaviour is out of your control, but whether or not *you* relate to them is completely in *your* control.

There is a special story attributed to the Buddha's life about dealing with people who are angry and who cause harm to others through their words.

THE ANGRY MAN

Once, the Buddha came to a small town to give a sermon. Most people of the village were very happy about the Buddha's presence and his teachings. However, one person was very displeased. He was angry at the Buddha and cursed him with rude and harsh words. He said, 'You have no right to teach others. You are just a fake.'

The Buddha did not react to these harsh insults at all. Instead, he calmly asked the angry man a question, 'If you get someone a gift and they do not accept it, who would the gift belong to?' The angry man was surprised at this question. He probably expected the Buddha to react to his provocative statements. He did not expect this calmness. He quietened down a bit and said, 'Well, it would belong to me because I got it in the first place.'

The Buddha then gently said, 'It is the same with your anger and insults. I do not accept them. They are all yours to keep.' This lesson was a great one for the man as well as for the spectators.

This story about the Buddha is such a simple and profound one. It communicates that we need not take the anger, taunts and insults hurled at us too personally. They are not about us. They are given to us and it is our choice whether to accept them or not. We can choose wisely not to engage with people who are bullying us.

This decision to not engage with the person bullying you of course takes courage, and once you set boundaries, there may be difficult consequences. We will learn how best to address those in the discussions that follow.

For now, let's see what Sarah could do to set a boundary. Sarah could try talking to Aditi and tell her that she will not tolerate this kind of behaviour. If Aditi does not respond to this and continues to bully her, Sarah can walk away from the friendship and stop hanging out with Aditi.

Reflection Space

What can you do to set some clear boundaries in your situation? Do you think calmly talking to the person is worth an attempt? Or do you think it is better to completely ignore or stop engaging with that person? Even if that person is part of your family or a close group—which means that it will be difficult to ignore them completely—can you at least stop engaging with them when they are bullying you? Write down your thoughts about what you can do.

4. Expect difficult consequences when standing up to bullies

Standing up to a bully can be followed by actions and consequences that are difficult to handle. The consequences can be in the form of them teasing you more, using new kinds of insults or trying new ways of making you miserable.

In Sarah's case, on being confronted, Aditi may refuse to change her behaviour or may even reject Sarah right away. She could also gossip about her with others, call her whiny, weak or oversensitive and make Sarah's life even more difficult.

At the very least, if they stop being friends, Sarah will need to deal with being alone for at least a while until she makes other friends.

Reflection Space

Are you worried about the consequences of standing up to the person who is bullying you? What consequences are possible in your situation? What are you most fearful of? Please use the space below to explore this.

---

5. Get ready to be courageous and strong

Once you have confronted the people bullying you, things can look worse before they get better. The teasing might get harsher or you might find yourself alone and left out because you stopped engaging with those who were bullying you.

You will need to be steady, strong and courageous. You are standing up for yourself. Be proud of it.

Be like a warrior. Not a warrior that fights with swords and weapons but a peaceful one that fights with the strength and the power of silence.

To do this, your mindfulness practice is going to be your biggest support. Since you are practising mindfulness, you know how to stay with yourself peacefully. Every day, that is exactly what you have been doing in your meditation practice. Staying with your breath or with your body sensations peacefully! You have learnt that life has some difficulties that are out of your control, and that you can stay with things that are not always very pleasant by staying present.

When you know how to stay quiet by yourself, being your own best friend, you are quite powerful. People can mock and tease all they want, but you are like a silent, strong rock. Unaffected and untouched.

In Sarah's case, she will have to stop engaging with Aditi. This will create a void in Sarah's life. Sarah will not only lose Aditi but the entire group of friends she is used to hanging out with. She will have to spend school breaks alone, maybe eat alone. Due to the fear of being alone, she may be tempted to put up with Aditi's unfair behaviour.

However, if Sarah reads this book and practises mindfulness and meditation, she will learn that while it is not easy to be alone, it is not so difficult either. She may meditate during her school breaks. She can try to stay mindful throughout this tough period. Instead of getting caught up in her mind's stories, she will try to observe sounds or if she is feeling emotional, she will observe her feelings with acceptance. She will also remind herself to be patient knowing that this tough period will end, new friendships will come along and things will change, as everything is impermanent.

Since she knows the difference between pleasure and happiness (page 23), she will also know that while staying with Aditi is pleasurable in the short term, it is harming her and not letting her be happy.

Reflection Space

How is your mindfulness practice going? Do you feel you can stay with yourself without distractions for a bit longer? Are you able to maintain silent times (page 35) in the day to be with yourself? Can you use the knowledge you have gained so far, and your meditation practice, to build courage and strength in you? What can you do to help yourself get stronger and more resilient?

_____

_____

_____

_____

6. Stay in tune with your wisdom

Any verbal bullying or teasing can have only so much power over you as you let it. The words may leave the mouth of the person who is bullying you, but to what extent they impact you will depend on how much you believe in them.

Bring to your mind the right understanding of bullying. Remind yourself that these teasing, harsh words uttered by the bully are emerging from a very unhappy mind. When we understand that the person who is bullying us is not more powerful or stronger but simply unhappy, we can respond to this person as we would respond to any unhappy person—with wisdom.

Responding with wisdom does not mean that we need to put up with mean and hurtful behaviour. It only means that we take the necessary actions like telling our parents and teachers, standing up to those who bully us or ignoring them, but we take these actions without creating negativity and judgement towards ourselves or the person who is bullying us.

We learn to see the other person as unhappy due to their own life circumstances and we turn our energy towards taking care of ourselves instead.

When you consult your inner wisdom and don't generate negativity and judgement in your mind towards the person who is bullying you, you save yourself from carrying a lot of ill-feeling.

Contemplate this: A person who is unhappy becomes a bully and tries to make you unhappy. If you allow your mind to create negative and hateful stories about them, your mind is now wallowing in unhappiness. They have successfully managed to include you in their unhappiness.

You don't want to internalize their unhappiness. So you set your boundaries and keep your distance, but you also try not to create negative judgements about them. Even if your mind is creating justifiably negative stories about a bully, it is still your mind that is getting filled with negativity. That is not what you want.

Sarah, too, will have to consult her inner wisdom similarly. She will have to remember that Aditi is acting out of her own unhappiness. Even if on the surface it seems like Aditi is very cool and has cool friends, she is not internally happy. She is troubled about something. Having this right understanding will be so powerful, that it will help Sarah do what needs to be done, without feeling terribly negative about Aditi.

Reflection Space

What does it mean for you to stay in tune with your wisdom? What would be a wise way to think about the situation you are in?

_____

_____

_____   _____

_____

7. Stay loving and compassionate

As we have seen earlier, compassion is like a soothing balm that can be put over a wound. When you are being bullied, you are hurt and wounded. You need this soothing balm of your compassion. Take care of yourself. Stay kind to yourself.

Even when you set a boundary, you are actually being compassionate to yourself. When you set boundaries for yourself and say no when needed, you do not spend too much time and energy trying to be around people who make you unhappy and doing things that are uncomfortable for you. That way you have energy left to be compassionate to others as well.

When you keep tolerating people who are mean, a lot of your energy gets used up in just bearing up with the bullying situation. Then you are so upset and caught up with the negativity of your own life that you have very little space to feel for others, to even think about them. You end up being obsessed with your own problems, and that's how you become less compassionate to others too.

Brené Brown, a researcher on vulnerability, shame and worthiness said, 'Daring to set boundaries is about having the courage to love ourselves, even when we risk disappointing others.' She believes people who keep strong boundaries are also among the most compassionate people.

Sometimes, people who are very wise, who have practised compassion for themselves and built a loving relationship with themselves, are able to actually practise compassion for those who hurt them too.

Such a wise person would look at someone who bullies them, realize how unhappy they are and wish for them, 'May you be well and happy. May you be free from suffering and pain.'

This may be very difficult for you at this juncture. However, as you follow the practices in this book, slowly you will find that your capacity to be kind to others and even to those who hurt you will increase.

Your regular metta practice (page 89) will help you with this greatly.

Reflection Space

How can you stay loving and compassionate to yourself while you deal with this difficult bullying situation? Have you been practising metta? How do you find it?

_____

_____

_____

_____

Here is an additional practice you can use if things get too overwhelming for you while dealing with bullying.

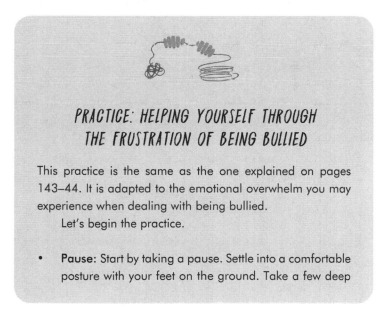

PRACTICE: HELPING YOURSELF THROUGH THE FRUSTRATION OF BEING BULLIED

This practice is the same as the one explained on pages 143–44. It is adapted to the emotional overwhelm you may experience when dealing with being bullied.

Let's begin the practice.

- **Pause:** Start by taking a pause. Settle into a comfortable posture with your feet on the ground. Take a few deep breaths until you feel a little calmer. Try and let go of thoughts about the person who is bullying you and instead, start to observe what emotion you are aware of at present.

- **Name the emotion:** Ask yourself what is it that you are feeling? Is it frustration, anger, helplessness or sadness?
- **Accept the emotion:** Allow yourself to fully feel this emotion. Accept that it is there right now. It is painful, but it is okay for it to be there.
- **Support yourself:** Stay kind to yourself. You are already hurt by another person. It's understandable that you feel this difficult emotion because bullying is so very painful to endure.

If you are feeling worked up, just walk slowly, feeling your feet on the ground. With your hands, make very slow pushing movements that create boundaries.

Push out with your hands towards the front and towards the side very slowly, all the while noticing how the gentle pushing movement makes you feel. While pushing, be very slow and deliberate, paying full attention to the movement. As you push, imagine that you are pushing everything a little away from yourself and creating space for yourself in which you can breathe.

When the movements help you to feel a bit settled, give yourself a hug. Stay mindful while hugging yourself. You need your own love at this moment. This kind of support will help you deal with the overwhelming feeling you are going through.

Do You Bully Others?

As it is important to recognize when we are being bullied, it is equally important to recognize when we bully others. No one believes that they could be bad or be a bully, but in our ignorance or even because we are pained in some way, we may actually be hurting others.

So, here is what you need to reflect on: do you tease others; make fun of people; ridicule others because they are too short, too tall, because they stammer, or for any other reason? Do you call others names, laugh when they are in trouble or actively pursue someone and say nasty things to them? Do you participate in a group that makes jokes about others, ridicules others, or in any way verbally or physically harms others? If yes, you are either actively bullying someone or at least participating in bullying.

It is also true that you can feel bullied in some situations and can still also bully others in a different situation. In fact, this is quite common.

Let us look at a possible scenario. Let's say you feel bullied by others in the school. You store up all that anger and come home. You have a younger sibling at home or even a friend in your building you play with. You now direct all your frustration at them. For instance, if your sibling asks you to teach them science, you tell them how they suck at science or how pathetic they are and tease them.

Now you become the bully, and all that applies to a bully applies to you too. You are unhappy, not at peace and you are trying to make yourself feel better by making others miserable. You are not a 'bad' person, not at all! But you are unhappy.

In the above situation, you are unhappy because you are angry and frustrated due to the bullying in school. You are carrying the frustration to your home and then directing the anger on to others. But there are also many other things that could make you upset, sad, frustrated and angry. Maybe you have a difficult relationship with your parents. Maybe you just don't feel good enough in some areas. Maybe you feel like no matter how hard you try, you are not appreciated. You don't know what to do with all the pent-up anger and frustration and you instead bully someone as a way of venting your frustration.

You start teasing people, making them feel small and inadequate—and that is your way of feeling better. You unconsciously think, 'I am not happy, so I will make others unhappy and miserable too.' This is the sad cycle of suffering or dukkha, which we spoke about earlier in the book (page 9). When we don't understand our own sadness and pain, we don't have any mindfulness and wisdom practice, we remain unhappy and make our environment and the people in it suffer too.

It is not that you are going to feel better in the long term by harming and laughing at others; you are only going to get some momentary or short-term release. Your own troubles and issues won't go away by bullying others. Instead, now you have expanded your circle of suffering. You have also made others suffer because of your suffering. And as a result, more people are unhappy.

This is the way all harm in the world spreads. Wars, angry mobs, violence against others, all of it exists because people do not pause to recognize and deal with their own pain. So, you see, bullying is a weak, unwise and mindless stand taken by people who are suffering.

Make the Wise Choice to Stop Bullying

Now, the great news is that every person who feels a desire to bully or harm others has a *choice*. A wise and mindful person will recognize the urge to hurt, belittle or ridicule others and will pause instead of giving in to that urge. They will turn inwards to observe how they are feeling. They will see that they are suffering and will try to stay with their own feelings with kindness and compassion.

You have a lot of help in this book if you really want to make a wise choice. Here is a suggestion: go through the practices in Part IV, which is an entire section dedicated to making friends with your feelings. Go through it again if you have merely skimmed through it earlier. Use the practices to observe what emotion you are really going through. What is the pain that is so unbearable for you, that it makes you want to hurt others? If you learn wisely to support that pain, to take care of yourself while you go through it, you may not want to push it on to others. Also, your own pain will start to lighten.

We all have angry, frustrated and not-so-great aspects within us. We also have the beautiful, gentle, compassionate and wise Buddha nature within us. What we choose to give energy to will decide what kind of people we are and what impact we have on the world around us.

Here is a beautiful story to help you with that:

THE FIGHT WITHIN

An old grandfather was once teaching his grandson about life.

'A fight is going on inside me,' he said to the boy. 'It is a terrible fight, and it is between two wolves. One is evil—he is anger, envy, regret, greed, arrogance, self-pity, guilt, resentment, inferiority, lies, false pride, superiority and ego. The other is good; he is joy, peace, love, hope, serenity, humility, kindness, benevolence, empathy, generosity, truth, compassion and faith. The same fight is going on inside you—and inside every other person, too.'

The grandson thought about it for a minute and then asked his grandfather, 'Which wolf will win?'

The grandfather replied, 'The one you feed.'

This simple story urges you to recognize that you have a choice. You can choose which aspect of yourself you want to strengthen.

It is like going to a gym to build some muscles. When people want to strengthen and build muscles of their arms, they exercise their arms; if they want to strengthen their leg muscles, they do squats and lunges and other leg exercises. Similarly, with the mind, whatever you repeatedly choose and exercise will be strengthened.

If you spend your energy on putting people down, hurting them, taking revenge and making yourself feel better by making others miserable, you will strengthen that mean, rude and bitter part of you.

Even if you feel like hurting someone, if instead of giving in to that urge, you instead turn towards yourself in kindness and understanding, you will strengthen the part of you that is loving, compassionate and kind. This is the part that will ultimately lead you to live more happily as a person.

Here are some practices from this book that will greatly help you:

PRACTICES FOR THOSE WHO TEND TO BULLY

1. **Metta practice (page 89):** Focus more on feeling kindness for yourself first. Just do the first part of the practice that involves visualizing yourself and being kind to yourself.

   Once you have practised this for a few days and you are able to feel more compassion and friendliness for yourself, add the second step of sending friendliness to the world.

   Once you have practised these two steps and feel comfortable with them, add the third step where you show compassion to those who are making you suffer and are difficult people in your life.

   If you practice like this, you will start feeling compassion for all people and your urge to bully them will definitely come down.

2. **Four steps to working with difficult feelings (pages 143–44):** This practice will help you deal with the

unhappiness and the unpleasant feelings you go through. Whenever you feel emotional, please visit this practice and go through it with kindness towards yourself.

3. **Gratitude as a way of life (page 42):** Try to notice one good thing about your life every day. When you are angry and you bully others, your mind can become wired to pick on everyone's negative traits. The practice of noticing and appreciating good things about life will change the mind's tendency. When the mind perceives fewer negatives, our life becomes naturally joyful.

Going through this book, trying to understand what is being said and practising regularly will not only help you reduce the tendency to bully others but also transform your own life into a happy one.

A poisonous plant that poisons others holds poison within it, and a flower that makes its environment fragrant is itself fragrant. It is not possible to smell rotten on the inside and make your environment fragrant, just as it is not possible to put poison into the environment without that poison being inside you.

We can only give to others what we truly have. If we are loving to ourselves, we become loving to others. If we are violent to others, we are unloving to ourselves and bitter within. This is how nature works.

With the right understanding, even an unwise tendency like bullying can become an opportunity to understand ourselves better.

PRACTICE SUMMARY

When a heavy object falls from a height on to the ground, two factors decide the impact of the collision. One factor is about the object—how heavy it is, its size and the height from which it falls. The other factor is about the quality of the ground. If the ground is hard, the impact is harder. If the ground is soft, the impact is weaker.

It is the same when we deal with difficult situations. They are like heavy objects and their nature is out of our control. However, we are like the ground. We can work to make it soft and receiving instead of hard and repelling. If we have a wise mind and a kind heart, then the intensity of the impact will be lower. We will be less affected.

You have gone through an entire part on how to deal with challenges all the while keeping yourself wise and kind. By now you know that this is possible only with regular practice.

Going forward, you can do just the practices laid out below on a regular basis. Try to increase the time duration of the practices gradually. You can do one practice each day, any time during the day that suits you.

1. **Breathing meditation (page 67)**: Do the breathing meditation practice for 10–15 minutes.
2. **Body scan practice (page 115)**: Do the body scan practice, either lying down or sitting for 15–20 minutes.

3. **Metta practice (page 89):** Do the metta practice for fifteen minutes. If you have been practising metta so far, try to add the third step of the practice, of giving metta to a difficult person, on a regular basis now.

You could additionally imbibe the below practices in your routine:

*   Practise gratitude for two minutes before you go to sleep every day.
*   Try to stay mindful throughout the day. Keep your awareness in the present all day, as often as possible.
*   Revisit the practice on working with feelings when you are dealing with difficult feelings or emotions. If the challenge you are going through is covered in the chapters in Part V, you can directly go to that chapter and use the concepts and practices included there.

THE PATH AHEAD

You have reached the end of the book, but this is only the beginning of this new way of being. Here onwards, your life will always be supported by your inner wisdom, which you have discovered. You will always be nourished by the silence and joy that is already within you.

If you have applied even some of the learnings from the book to your life, you are already on your way to becoming your own best friend.

The path laid out in this book is the path of the gentle and peaceful warrior. Just as a warrior fights against that which is evil on the outside, a mindful warrior fights against the unhappy tendencies of self-obsession, fear, greed and pleasure-seeking on the inside.

The most important quality a warrior needs is the quality of courage. Turning inwards and changing your perspective and habits also needs tremendous courage. You need courage to resist the stories spun by the mind, to choose peace and happiness over pleasure, to try again even when you are unsuccessful, to face your fears, and to accept and stay kind to people even when you know they have flaws or are unkind to you.

This is a gentle kind of courage, a peaceful kind of war. There is no aggression here. Instead, all the while, the sunshine of kindness and compassion is illuminating your way.

Through your mindfulness practice, this courage has already started growing within you and will only gain strength as you practise regularly. When your intention is to live a life of wisdom and peace, nature will support you and give you many opportunities to grow.

Don't think of this book as something you have finished reading. Instead, think of it as a guide, a friend that you will always keep nearby and refer to whenever you need it. Read it little by little again. Make the practices given in the book a part of your life. Revisit parts of the book that can help you when you are going through a difficult situation.

So, go forth, you gentle and peaceful warrior, and live your life mindfully, happily and joyfully.

May you be your own best friend. May you be happy. May you be well and full of joy and peace.

REFERENCES

1. 'Research Shows That Mindfulness Is the Secret to Happiness'. The Mindfulness Summit. https://themindfulnesssummit.com/sessions/secret-to-happinessmindfulness-research/#happiness-research.
2. Crego, Antonio, José Ramón Yela, María Ángeles Gómez-Martínez, Pablo Riesco-Matías, and Cristina Petisco-Rodríguez. 'Relationships between Mindfulness, Purpose in Life, Happiness, Anxiety, and Depression: Testing a Mediation Model in a Sample of Women'. Int J Environ Res Public Health, 18 (3): 925 (2021), https://www.ncbi.nlm.nih.gov/pmc/articles/PMC7908241/.
3. https://www.azquotes.com/author/17650-Sri_Nisargadatta_Maharaj.
4. Trí, Quant. 'The story of the angry man'. The Buddha Journey. 30 September 2013. http://buddhajourney.net/the-story-of-the-angry-man/.
5. Brown, Brené. 'Brené Brown: 3 Ways to Set Boundaries'. O, The Oprah Magazine, September 2013 issue; also available on Oprah.com: https://www.oprah.com/spirit/how-to-set-boundaries-brene-browns-advice.
6. Honorato, B., N. Caltabiano and A.R. Clough. 'From trauma to incarceration: exploring the trajectory in a qualitative study in male prison inmates from north Queensland, Australia'. Health Justice, 4, 3 (2016). https://healthandjusticejournal.biomedcentral.com/articles/10.1186/s40352-016-0034-x.
7. Thomas, Liji Dr. 'Prisoner Post Traumatic Stress'. News-Medical.Net. Last updated on 27 February 2019. https://www.news-medical.net/health/Prisoner-Post-Traumatic-Stress.aspx.
8. 'Setting in Motion the Wheel of the Dhamma'. BuddhaSasana. https://www.budsas.org/ebud/ebsut001.htm.
9. Thera, Soma. 'The Way of Mindfulness: Satipatthana Sutta and Its Commentary'. https://www.accesstoinsight.org/lib/authors/soma/wayof.html.
10. 'Bullying'. Wikipedia. Last edited on 22 October 2021. https://en.wikipedia.org/wiki/Bullying.
11. Palmo, Jetsunma Tezin. Cave in the Snow: A Western Woman's Quest for Enlightenment. New Delhi: Bloomsbury Publishing India Private Limited, 1999, new edition.
12. Rinpoche, Yongey Mingyur, and Eric Swanson. The Joy of Living: Unlocking the Secret and Science of Happiness. New York: Harmony, 2008.
13. Hanh, Thich Nhat. Planting Seeds: Practicing Mindfulness with Children. California: Parallax Press, 2007.
14. Maharaj, Sri Nisargadatta. I am That: Talks with Sri Nisargadatta Maharaj. Mumbai: Chetana Private Ltd, 2003, revised edition.
15. Hanh, Thich Nhat. Old Path White Clouds: Walking in the Footsteps of the Buddha. Full Circle Publishing, 2017, nineteenth edition.
16. Hanh, Thich Nhat. The Heart of Understanding: Commentaries on the Prajnaparamita Heart Sutra. California: Parallax Press, 2005.
17. Willard, Christopher. Mindfulness for Teen Anxiety: A Workbook for Overcoming Anxiety at Home, at School, and Everywhere Else. California: New Harbinger Publications, 2014.
18. Saltzman, Amy. A Still Quiet Place: A Mindfulness Program for Teaching Children and Adolescents to Ease Stress and Difficult Emotions. California: New Harbinger Publications, 2016.

ACKNOWLEDGEMENTS

I am deeply grateful to all the revered gurus, who I have read, whose direct teachings I have heard in retreats and courses, and who have made it possible for me to internalize the teachings of wisdom to write this book: Ramana Maharishi, Venerable Geshe Dorji Damdul, Swami Sarvapriyananda, Venerable Mingyur Rinpoche, S.N. Goenkaji, Venerable Robina Courtin, Venerable Dhamma Dipaji, Venerable Tenzin Palmo, Papaji, Mooji, Om Swami and so many others.

I sincerely thank Raja Selvam, founder of Integral Somatic Psychotherapy, for teaching me to make friends with my body and discover the immense healing potential it has.

I thank my editor Arpita Nath, for approaching me with a plan for a book for pre-teens and teens on the subject of mindfulness, when I had neither contemplated writing a book nor looked at creating resources for this specific age group. Arpita, you helped me pleasantly surprise myself.

I deeply appreciate Ram Mantravadi, for being the constant wisdom presence around me, for being the critic, friend and guide that everyone on the path needs, and for shaking me out of my planned schedule to give the book its due importance and for helping me simplify it.

I deeply thank my friends who are my sangha and have toiled with me on this book: Jogendra Dasani, for being my first-draft editor and a serial motivator; Ravi Chander Ande and Natasha Nair, for spending days minutely scanning chunks of the book to suggest a better sounding word, a better approach, a clearer sentence; and Tejal Shah, for believing in my work, potential and lovingly connecting me to the resources I needed.

I have to thank my entire Inner Space team for generously allowing me space to write even while they accommodated my absence at work and managed everything so very smoothly.

Finally and most importantly, I would like to thank my family: my sisters, for believing in the way of wisdom, being co-meditators and a huge wall of love and support; and my mother, for being a powerful woman who lives life believing nothing is impossible. Her energy runs through me and has made this book possible.

REFLECTION SPACE

_____
_____
_____
_____
_____
_____
_____
_____
_____
_____
_____
_____
_____
_____
_____
_____
_____
_____
_____
_____
_____
_____